IF THE FOUNDATIONS ARE DESTROYED

Biblical Principles and Civil Government

K. ALAN SNYDER

If The Foundations Are Destroyed
Biblical Principles and Civil Government
by K. Alan Snyder

Printed in the United States of America

Library of Congress Catalog Card Number: 93-85596
ISBN 9781615799381

www.xulonpress.com

DEDICATION

To all my students, past and present, who encouraged me that I have written something worthwhile. May it always bear fruit in your lives.

ACKNOWLEDGMENTS

This book is the fruit of many years of teaching and learning. It is also the result of *re*teaching and *re*learning, because I went through a difficult time in my life when I questioned everything I had learned. I emerged from that period with a greater appreciation for God's love and patience. Therefore, the first and highest acknowledgment goes to Him.

Verna Hall and Rosalie Slater of the Foundation for American Christian Education introduced me to the Principle Approach in 1977. Miss Hall poured out her life researching America's Christian history. Many owe her an inestimable debt. Miss Slater, who walked away from a doctoral program in education when she realized it was sowing the wrong seeds, devoted the rest of her life to the application of Biblical principles to education. Her work continues to reap eternal rewards.

My wife, Jan, who works as a computer consultant, provided the most practical assistance, bailing me out of numerous computer glitches (human glitches, actually). Without her help, I might have remained in a state of word-processed despair. Some of us spend a significant proportion of our time thinking about principles and ideas, but we would be lost without those who make sure that those principles and ideas are put into a proper format for others to read. She deserves a greater reward than I can ever offer.

TABLE OF CONTENTS

PREFACE

C hristians sometimes don't know what to think about
civil government. There are extremes into which we
can fall. One group may believe that nothing less than a
theocracy can legitimately be called "Christian" government, while another holds the opinion that Christians
should have nothing to do with political activity because
it takes our minds off the more important matters of the
Spirit.

At one point in my intellectual and spiritual development, I concluded that the authority issue was so dominant that any resistance to civil authority was wrong.
I even thought, in my spiritual youth, that perhaps the
only way the United States could "make things right"
would be to go back under the authority of the British
government.

What follows is not an extremist book, although secularists may deem it so. Committed secularists attach
the extremist label to anyone who makes a connection between Biblical beliefs and civil government. By
responding in this manner, however, they reveal more
clearly their own extremism, based on the view that
God should be omitted from everything outside the
walls of the church. This book, instead, is an attempt to
explain the proper balance in the relationship between

the Kingdom of God and the kingdoms of man. I believe, without apology, that Biblical principles apply to all areas of life; therefore, it would be wrong to exclude them from our understanding and practice of civil government. There is a hunger for this perspective. Although my primary audience has been my students, I have taken advantage of a number of opportunities to speak to more general Christian audiences about the principles enunciated in this book. The response always has been positive. Christians are awakening to their civic responsibilities. One year, I was honored to speak to approximately four hundred Christian activists in Tennessee on the day that the Tennessee legislature opened. These awakened Christians were there to pray for their legislators and to talk with them about policy concerns. It is a joy to be able to participate in such a reawakening.

Any reawakening, though, must be coupled with true reformation of thought and life. If Christians are to make a difference in American society, their walk must match their talk. We truly must be lights in a dark world. For those who are attempting to be lights, I hope this book provides some clues for knowing how to walk in the darkness that surrounds us.

INTRODUCTION

A troubled Rev. Jedidiah Morse stood in his Charlestown, Massachusetts, pulpit on 25 April 1799. He was deeply concerned for the future of the young American republic. France had just gone through a bloody revolution, an event that had triggered a torrent of emotions in the United States. Men who had worked and fought together to give birth to America and her Constitution no longer spoke to one another. The anti-christian emphasis of the French Revolution seemingly had crossed the Atlantic and was beginning to infect Rev. Morse's new nation, a nation he considered a Christian republic. On that day in 1799 he issued a warning to his congregation:

> Our dangers are of two kinds, those which affect our religion, and those which affect our government. They are, however, so closely allied that they cannot, with propriety, be separated. The foundations which support the interests of Christianity, are also necessary to support a free and equal government like our own.... To the kindly influence of Christianity we owe that degree of civil freedom, and political and social happiness which mankind now enjoy. In proportion as the genuine effects of Christianity are diminished in any nation, either through unbelief, or the corruption of its

doctrines, or the neglect of its institutions; in the same proportion will the people of that nation recede from the blessings of genuine freedom, and approximate the miseries of complete despotism.... Whenever the pillars of Christianity shall be overthrown, our present republican forms of government, and all the blessings which flow from them, must fall with them.[1]

The danger was averted in 1799. In fact, the first half of the nineteenth century witnessed the most extensive Christian revival in American history. Yet Rev. Morse's concern was valid. The country could have gone the other direction. Only a revitalized Christian faith kept it on the right path.

Morse's text for that sermon was Psalm 11:3: "If the foundations are destroyed, what can the righteous do?" If that text and his concerns were appropriate for his day, they are doubly appropriate for America in the twenty-first century. Rev. Morse, if he could compare the problems his America faced with the problems America faces today, would undoubtedly accept the premise that the danger has multiplied in the two hundred-plus years since he spoke his words of warning. If the foundations were in danger of being destroyed in 1799, how much more so now?

Yet the answer for modern America is the same as it was for 1799 America. Foundations must be rebuilt. Christian principles must be reestablished. We must return to God the Source.

CHAPTER 1

GOD THE SOURCE

C hristians should not have to debate the idea that God is the source of everything. We acknowledge Him as creator of the earth and all it contains. We hold to the concept that man is His special creation made in His image, possessing intellect, emotion, and the power of moral choice. We even base all our beliefs on a written document called the Bible, declaring it to be the Word of God. If the Bible is the actual expression of the thoughts and commandments of God, it should apply to every part of our lives; Jesus Christ should be Lord in all things. Sadly, this often is not true.

God has given us a guidebook to all of life, yet Christians sometimes set up a wall of separation between what might be considered "spiritual" matters and those that are called "secular." There is a particular reluctance among some evangelicals to consider the Bible as a guide into a proper understanding of civil government. Yes, they say, it provides the moral instruction we need to operate civil government, but surely not the pattern or blueprint for a *type* of government in harmony with the way God has made all things. To believe that God has a particular type of government that He prefers above all others, they caution, would be a mixing of the spiritual and the secular. God is not concerned about the structure of government; all He cares about is how we conduct ourselves whatever the structure. At least, that is the main thrust of the argument.

Yet to promote the notion that God doesn't care about governmental structure excludes one aspect of His creation from His oversight. A barrier is erected between the Word of God and man's political theories, as if to say that it is all up to man to decide what is best in government. Does God really have nothing to say about this? Didn't He create man? Isn't it more than possible that He knows best how to regulate man in society? It is understandable why nonchristians exclude the Bible from the marketplace of political ideas, but why do Christians often take the same approach?

One objection to using the Bible as a political textbook is the belief that the most important Biblical message is personal salvation. Concentration on other matters, especially politics, may detract from the primary message. Government, critics say, is a temporal affair, and we ought to have our eyes on the eternal, not the temporal. Implicit in the objection many voice toward the linking of the Bible and politics is the belief that, in some unique way, politics is a particularly dirty and unchristian activity.

There certainly can be no disagreement on the priority of personal salvation. Christians at times have devoted so much energy to the political arena that priorities have been reversed.[1] There is a temptation to rely too much on political solutions. A political crusade, which may begin with a solid Christian foundation, can alter itself in such a way that the Christian roots become secondary, indeed virtually nonexistent. That is a danger of which all Christians should be aware, but is the *tempta-*

tion to reverse priorities a good enough reason to abstain from all political involvement? Can't Christians develop a Biblical view of politics and government and bring some influence to bear on public policy?

The answer to that question forces us to go back to the word *salvation*. Just what does it mean in all of its implications? In personal terms it denotes a turning away from sin, a turning toward Christ for forgiveness of sin, and the beginning of a new way of life, what the Bible calls a new creation. This new creation, or new man, is supposed to submit his life to God for a constant renewing of the mind and purifying of old habit patterns. He is being remade into the image of Christ. Without the renewal and new Christlike habit patterns, one can legitimately wonder if salvation has occurred.

If real salvation has taken place, this new man, with his mind continually renewed, will start to look at all things through the eyes of Christ. And if he is open to the leading of the Holy Spirit, won't he want to extend Christian influence into every part of society? If not, then again it may be reasonable to question his conversion experience.

Did God give over the world to Satan? Is this no longer God's territory? Other books have talked about the dominion mandate God gave man when he was first created. A brief summary is all that is necessary here.

Genesis declares that God made man in His own image. Then God blessed man and made him the ruler over all the rest of creation.[2] Most evangelicals accept this. Then man fell. After the fall, some say, God revoked the dominion mandate. Yet God spoke to Noah in much the same terms when He gave him instructions after the Flood. Although sin had destroyed the pre-Flood world, God still expected the "new" human race to take charge again.[3]

Jesus expected His followers to exhibit leadership when He told them they were to be the salt of the earth and the light of the world.[4] It is difficult to be salt and light if one refuses to help determine the government of society. Does it make much sense to turn everything over to nonchristians and hope for the best?

Yet the Bible does clearly call Satan the ruler of this world, doesn't it? Jesus gave Satan that very title.[5] Paul writes about the god of this world who has blinded the minds of the unbelieving and, in two other pastoral letters, refers to Satan as the prince of the power of the air.[6]

We must read these verses in context. Satan only has power over the minds of the "unbelieving," and he is prince only over those Paul terms "the sons of disobedience." When Jesus acknowledged Satan as ruler of this world, He went on to decree that this "ruler" was about to be cast out of his illegitimate kingdom through the Son of God's death and resurrection. In every case, it is evident that the power of God is stronger than the power of Satan, and that if Christians walk in obedience they can take dominion over the designs of the enemy. Consequently, the argument that the dominion mandate no longer applies does not pass a Biblical examination. The concern that political involvement may take our eyes off the primary Biblical message of personal salvation, while noteworthy, is not sufficient to keep Christians out of governmental affairs. As long as *God's* priorities remain *our* priorities we are free (indeed commanded) to extend His lordship to every area of life.

Another possible reason why Christians avoid declaring "Thus saith the Lord" in government and politics is that it may seem arrogant. Who are we to say that we really know the mind of the Lord on this issue? After all, didn't the prophet Isaiah warn,

"For My thoughts are not your thoughts, neither are your ways My ways," declares the Lord. "For as the heavens are higher than the earth, so are My ways higher than your ways, and My thoughts than your thoughts."[7]

And didn't the apostle Paul tell the Corinthians,

For who among men knows the thoughts of a man except the spirit of the man, which is in him? Even so the thoughts of God no one knows except the Spirit of God.[8]

The very next verse, however, clearly states,

Now we have received, not the spirit of the world, but the Spirit who is from God, that we might know the things freely given to us by God.[9]

As Christians, we have access to the Holy Spirit, the same Spirit who is part of the triune God, and who knows all things that the Father and Son know. This same Spirit lives inside us, longing to give us knowledge, under-standing, and wisdom. This brings us to the very crux of the matter.

Knowledge, Understanding, and Wisdom

God is the source of all knowledge, understanding, and wisdom. Nearly every Christian will say that from a sincere heart. Yet in practice it is easy to substitute the world's knowledge, understanding, and wisdom for God's, without realizing we are doing it. We need to examine the relationship between our speech and our actions in this critical realm. To do so, we must first reflect on the mean-ings of the words *knowledge, understanding, and wisdom.*

There are distinct differences among these terms, as well as two types of each—Christian versus worldly.

Knowledge is a word that is often used in a broad sense. When used in that way, it takes on some characteristics of understanding and wisdom. Therefore, it is essential to refer to its narrowest definition to make the distinctions clear.

Strictly speaking, knowledge is the accumulation or collection of data or information. A person may be a virtual storehouse of facts. He may astound others with his ability to recall vast amounts of information or statistics. Perhaps he has memorized significant portions of the Bible. But the accumulation of facts alone does not automatically lend itself to understanding.

A first-grader may "learn" that 2+2=4. A high school student may be told that America's founders signed the Declaration of Independence in 1776. Fine facts, but what do they mean? Dustin Hoffman, in the movie *Rain Man*, portrayed an autistic individual with tremendous intellectual powers. The only problem was that he was out of touch with reality. He had no concept of the value of his statistical information. Knowledge—pure factual knowledge—is not enough.

Understanding, defined as comprehension of the real state of things, must join with knowledge. To understand something is to know why these facts are significant.

The first-grader who "learned" that 2+2=4 simply may have memorized information. There may be no connection between this new information and the real world. True understanding occurs only when the first-grader comprehends that two "things" added to two other "things" make four "things." The same applies to the high-schooler who "learns" that the founders signed the Declaration of Independence in 1776. Understanding is possible only when that fact is interwoven with a clear presentation of the problems in the Revolutionary era, the truths contained in the Declaration, and the impact it had on society at that time, and even today.

The third concept is wisdom, which introduces a new element: moral choice. The definition of wisdom is the right use or exercise of that which we understand. This attribute does not come easily to man. I contend that man, without God, stumbles upon wisdom primarily by accident. Most of man's wisdom is the result of experiencing what does or does not work. Even so, we continue to repeat the foolish practices of earlier civilizations—to our detriment.

Clearly then, a true grasp of knowledge, understanding, and wisdom requires distinctions. But another dimension must be added—the world's standard for knowledge, understanding, and wisdom versus the Christian standard. What does the Bible say about these three words? Actually, the Bible says so much about knowledge, understanding, and wisdom that there is no way to present it all within this chapter. Yet I will attempt a few observations.

"The fear of the Lord is the beginning of knowledge," Proverbs informs us.[10] Later in the same book the writer reminds us, "The fear of the Lord is the beginning of wisdom, and the knowledge of the Holy One is understanding."[11] These verses seem to indicate that the distinctions mentioned above are consistent with Biblical teaching. The starting place for knowledge of any type is first to have a knowledge of God. Knowledge of God helps bring understanding; wisdom is available only through the same fear of the Lord that brought knowledge of Him in the first place. The message is plain: whether one focuses on knowledge, understanding, or wisdom, one must *begin* with God the Source. That theme can be found throughout the Scriptures.

The theme is expounded first in Deuteronomy when Moses reminds the people how completely God is to rule their thoughts:

> And these words, which I am commanding you today, shall be on your heart; and you shall teach them diligently to your sons and shall talk of them when you sit in your house and when you walk by the way and when you lie down and when you rise up. And you shall bind them as a sign on your hand and they shall be as frontals on your forehead. And you shall write them on the doorposts of your house and on your gates.[12]

According to these instructions, the knowledge of God should surround people at all times and in all places. There is no division between sacred and secular; all of life is God's domain. The psalmist is quite direct when he admonishes,

> Pay heed, you senseless among the people; and when will you understand, stupid ones? He who planted the ear, does He not hear? He who formed the eye, does He not see? He who chastens the nations, will He not rebuke, even He who teaches man knowledge? The Lord knows the thoughts of man, that they are a mere breath.[13]

These verses sound a clarion call for people to stop being "stupid," and to gain understanding through the knowledge of God. God made the ears and eyes, yet we still try to exclude Him from what we hear and see. He is the One "who teaches man knowledge"; He is the source. And when God looks at man's attempts to think on his own, without acknowledging His ways, He calls such thinking "a mere breath," something without any real substance.

Instruction and warning are both incorporated into the last chapter of Ecclesiastes:

> The words of wise men are like goads, and masters of these collections are like well-driven nails; they are given by one Shepherd. But beyond this, my son, be warned: the writing of many books is endless, and excessive devotion to books is wearying to the body. The conclusion, when all has been heard is: fear God and keep His commandments, because this applies to every person. Because God will bring every act to judgment, everything which is hidden, whether it is good or evil.[14]

While extolling wisdom, the writer reminds the reader that true wisdom comes only from one Shepherd, i.e., God. He then cautions man against the single-minded pursuit of knowledge for the sake of knowledge alone and reminds man that the fear of God is what life is all about.

The prophet Jeremiah, while inviting the faithless Jews to repent, relays this promise from God:

> Then I will give you shepherds after My own heart, who will feed you on knowledge and understanding.[15]

Again the connection is made between God and real knowledge and understanding. Shepherds include more than pastors; teachers shepherd students, and they must first have God's heart to transmit the type of knowledge and understanding God wants for His people. Implicit in this verse is the need for students (of whatever age) to be taught only by those who will teach them God's ways. The heart of God is conspicuously absent in most education.

Jesus, in the New Testament, said of the Pharisees,

> Let them alone; they are blind guides of the blind. And if a blind man guides a blind man, both will fall into a pit.[16]

Although the Pharisees claimed to be God's spokesmen, they had substituted man's understanding for God's. This is particularly important for Christians to recognize. It is not just the "world" out there somewhere that is undermining the Word of God; too often Christians, especially in Christian schools and colleges, look to academic studies and research first, and try to make the Bible fit the conclusions of those studies. Instead, they should be giving priority to the Word of God and analyzing all human endeavors in the light of His truth.

Probably the most powerful indictment of the attempt to banish God from human intellectual endeavor is found in Romans. The Apostle Paul virtually explodes against people who deliberately try to divorce God from His creation.

"For the wrath of God is revealed from heaven against all ungodliness and unrighteousness of men, who suppress the truth in unrighteousness," he declares, "because that which is known about God is evident within them; for God made it evident to them." He continues, "For since the creation of the world His invisible attributes, His eternal power and divine nature, have been clearly seen, being understood through what has been made, so that they are without excuse." Paul then concludes:

> For even though they knew God, they did not honor Him as God, or give thanks; but they became futile in their speculations, and their foolish heart was darkened. Professing to be wise, they became fools, and exchanged the glory of the incorruptible God for an

image in the form of corruptible man and of birds and four-footed animals and crawling creatures.... For they exchanged the truth of God for a lie, and worshiped and served the creature rather than the Creator, who is blessed forever. Amen.[17]

Men already know who God is, says Paul. They have to try very hard to "suppress the truth." They refuse to give Him the honor He is due and the result is that they become fools. They waste their time in "futile speculations" and end up believing lies because they do not want to acknowledge God as the source of everything.

The first three chapters of I Corinthians form a treatise on the distinction between godly and worldly knowledge, understanding, and wisdom. Paul gives considerable attention to the contrast between the human wisdom of the Greeks and God's wisdom. The Greeks come out the losers. "Has not God made foolish the wisdom of the world?" Paul asks.[18] God's wisdom is "not of this age, nor of the rulers of this age, who are passing away"; it is a wisdom "which none of the rulers of this age has understood."[19] But the Christian, affirms Paul, has "the mind of Christ" and can understand the thoughts of God.[20] "The Lord knows the reasonings of the [worldly] wise, that they are useless."[21] Nowhere in the Scriptures can a firmer basis be found for asserting that knowledge of God is the best ground for declaring precisely what constitutes real understanding and wisdom.

If any doubt remains on this subject, all that is necessary is to turn to Colossians, where Paul speaks of his hopes for the Laodicean Christians:

That their hearts may be encouraged, having been knit together in love, and attaining to all the wealth that comes from the full assurance of understanding, resulting in a true knowledge of God's mystery, that is,

Christ Himself, in whom are hidden all the treasures of wisdom and knowledge.[22]

In Christ are hidden "all the treasures of wisdom and knowledge." We may not possess all wisdom and knowledge, but we know where to find the Source for everything we need to know. We may not always agree on what constitutes God's knowledge, understanding, and wisdom in a particular area of thought or practice, but we all have access to the same Spirit, and as He develops a unity of spirit among us, we may move steadily toward a unity of belief.[23]

The Christian community has not achieved unity of belief in its understanding of government. I do not hold the utopian view that complete unanimity is achievable. I do believe, however, that we can come closer to unanimity if we acknowledge certain basic truths.

Biblical Principles

A principle is the source or origin of anything; it is a *general truth*, that is, a truth that is so broad and sweeping that many other truths can be considered offshoots of it. The idea of general truths that apply to all of society formerly had wide endorsement in America. The Declaration of Independence speaks of self-evident truths and goes on to list some basic rights God has given man.

One can legitimately question whether American society today still adheres to an unalterable body of truth. The onset of evolutionary philosophy and the pragmatism to which it has given birth have led us to think more in terms of expediency than principle. People sacrifice principles to that which is less troublesome. Standing on principle can be wearying when no one else seems to care or understand what you are doing. Yet God calls on Christians to make His principles the foundation of all they say and do.

Christians get in trouble when they conform to the world's thinking and ignore principles. They are tempted not to cause waves, forgetting that the world already is a turbulent place and that men are seeking—whether they realize it or not—for the stability of fixed principles. These principles can come only from the Christians, from those who base all decisions upon Biblical truth.

The problem lies with the question, "Just what are these principles, or general truths, that should form the basis for all we think?" The purpose of the succeeding chapters is to explain what these principles *might be*. Each person must decide for himself whether these principles are adequately supported Biblically. Yet even for those who may see other principles beyond the ones mentioned here, it is my fervent hope that the principles discussed in this book may at least provide a starting point for further exploration. At the very least, if these principles are acknowledged to be consistent with a Biblical worldview, they will provide the beginning of a basis for unity. The principles to be covered are:

1) Individuality
2) Self-Government
3) Property
4) Unity and Union
5) Christian Character
6) Biblical Form of Government
7) Sowing and Reaping

These seven principles have application to all of life, with government and politics being only one such application. Yet if understood and accepted, they will transform one's concepts of government; we could see a renewal of Biblical government in this country.

CHAPTER 2

INDIVIDUALITY: THE CORNERSTONE

I was in high school. There was a new sense of freedom. We were now mature enough to leave school grounds during lunch if we chose to eat elsewhere. Contemplation of the cafeteria food often led us to other sources of sustenance. I was walking back with a friend from a nearby deli during one of those lunchtimes. Ahead of us on the sidewalk, coming our way, were two girls. They were still too far away for us to see clearly, so they could not recognize us either. When we finally got close enough, one of them said, "We knew who both of you were even when we couldn't see your faces." Then she divulged the secret: it was the way we walked. There was a distinctiveness about our manner of walking that gave a clue to our identities even when they couldn't discern our facial features. She didn't know it, but she had just explained one facet of God's principle of individuality.

I grew up in the Lutheran church. My most poignant memories of those early years are of the sensation of God's magnificence, communicated primarily through organ music inspired by Bach (I didn't know then that

Bach wrote his works for the glory of God) and the effect of being surrounded by stained-glass windows. Each window told a story and each was comforting and terrifying in its own way—terrifying in the wholesome sense known as "the fear of the Lord." To some extent those windows shaped my concept of God; I began to see Him as worthy of my veneration and obedience. Others did not feel the same awe. Why was I so affected by these windows? Again, it was the principle of individuality.

The Biblical concept of individuality can be stated succinctly: God has created all things distinct and unique and for specific purposes. He has given an identity to all parts of His creation, whether material objects, animals, or the world of human beings.

Individuality is the cornerstone for all the other principles in this book. A cornerstone is the primary stone in a building, imbedded into the foundation as the starting point for the entire structure. In the spiritual sense, a cornerstone is something fundamentally important to a system of belief, without which the understanding of other truths is weakened. Individuality serves that function as the cornerstone principle in a network of Biblical principles that should guide us in all our thinking.

The most significant aspect of individuality is the recognition that it is a gift from God. Some notions of individuality are disconnected from God the Source. People may see individuality in the world, yet miss the spiritual impact God wants to make through the discovery of His creation.

Individuality in the Physical World

God directs the attention of all men to individuality in the physical world, a world designed to be an instrument through which men understand the power of the Creator. As King David exclaims:

> The heavens are telling of the glory of God; and their expanse is declaring the work of His hands. Day to day pours forth speech, and night to night reveals knowledge. There is no speech, nor are there words; their voice is not heard. Their sound has gone out through all the earth, and their utterances to the end of the world.[1]

This passage sounds contradictory. The creation "speaks," yet there are no words; it declares God's handiwork, yet there is no voice. No voice is *heard*, yet the *sound* has reverberated throughout the earth, and utterances have gone around the world. It is a wonderfully poetic way of describing how God works in the hearts and minds of men even without another person to tell them what they are beginning to understand. This Psalm has the same message that Paul preached in Romans when he told the church that the world rejects the knowledge of God through its rejection of His creation.[2]

How does the physical world tell of the works of His hands? It speaks volumes about the person and character of God through recognition of the individuality of the creation—the distinctness, uniqueness, and identity He has given to the individual parts—and the specific purposes for each part.

Many years ago I took my son to the Smithsonian Institution, and we entered a large room filled with display cases. In these cases were samples of rocks of all types. There were igneous, sedimentary, and metamorphic types. Within each classification there were dozens of distinct groupings. Within each of these groupings, there was astounding variety. I never knew so many different kinds of amethysts existed. An amethyst itself is just one type of quartz. And each rock in that room had a purpose. Men had used each type to serve some specific function. Probably the most fascinating piece of information that day was the acknowledgment on a sign in the room that the collection we were admiring constituted only a fraction—approximately 5 percent—of the entire Smithsonian rock collection. That discovery was remarkable.

On another occasion, my son and I took a walk through the woods behind our house. He had become intrigued with the varieties of trees in the world and had brought home a book from the library with pictures and descriptions of almost every kind of tree imaginable. Our little expedition was for the purpose of identifying the trees in our woods. So, with book in hand, we set out to explore and discover.

I am positive that I learned more than he did. I had never given the variety of trees much thought, but as we walked, we not only identified different types of trees, but we came face to face with the incredible variety within each type. I knew there were many oaks in our woods, but I had no idea that these oaks were divided into white, red, and black oaks. Later I found out that there are about four hundred fifty species of oaks in the world, and that oaks are merely one genus in the beech family of trees. Further research revealed that oaks are used for a variety of purposes: ornamentation; the manufacture of ink; commercial cork; dyes; and, of course, for timber.

We even see individuality in the changing of the seasons and in the various types of weather in each season. Each snowflake is individual and unique. There is purpose in spring, summer, fall, and winter—for farmers certainly, but also in regulating the lives of those who don't engage in that particular occupation.

The most obvious conclusion one should reach when considering the physical creation is that God must be a God who loves variety. If creation had been left up to a man (especially if I had been that man) the world would have been the repository of something called the "generic flower" or the "generic tree." God wasn't satisfied with making a generic anything. He wanted the creation to reveal something about Himself. I believe it does.

Historically, it is possible to look at the physical world through a Biblical perspective and see the hand of God at work in the shaping of the continents. If we believe that God creates with a purpose, then it is not illogical to believe that the land masses are situated in such a way to help accomplish His purposes.

God planted mankind primarily in the northern continents. There are advantages to man in these locations. These continents have temperate climates and experience regular changes of seasons, allowing for variety, and challenging man to plan ahead. They also have many coastal indentations and many islands just off the coasts. Excellent harbors meet man's need for trade and commerce.

The southern continents are entirely different. Approximately two-thirds of Australia is desert. The most dominant geographic feature in northern Africa is the Sahara Desert (what one person has described as the world's largest beach). Central Africa is primarily tropical. The same tropical feature can be found in South America, home of the Amazon Jungle.

The temperate zones for both Africa and South America coincide with the narrowing of the land masses; most of the land in each continent is located in the tropical or subtropical areas. The oppressive heat and humidity of the tropics are not naturally conducive to man's activity—one must work hard to overcome the desire to rest in the heat of the day. Vegetation and animal life dominate; man is almost an intruder in some areas.

God's love of variety shows not only in the distinct physical differences between the northern and southern continents, but in the individuality of each of the northern continents as well. Although all three—Asia, Europe, and North America—have been center stage for man's historical drama, each has served a different purpose in God's plans for man.

Asia is the Continent of Origins. It is the largest continent and has the greatest geographic contrasts and most impressive barriers, the Himalayan Mountains being the most prominent. Its size and barriers served effectively for the development of distinct civilizations, or races, of people.

The earliest civilizations began in Mesopotamia (the Fertile Crescent), the Indus Valley, and in China. Tremendous barriers isolated these civilizations. They developed almost independently from one another. The one major civilization not included in these regions was Egypt in northern Africa, but that civilization, for all practical purposes, was Mesopotamian in orientation, located at the extreme western end of the Fertile Crescent.

Why did God want this variety when it seems that each civilization developed ideas contrary to Biblical truth? This was not God's fault; it has to do with the will of man. Men had the true knowledge of God as they dispersed from Babel. They simply corrupted the truth that God had given them.

God hoped to reestablish truth. He called Abram out of Ur and gave him the promise of descendants, both physical and spiritual. He led Moses and Joshua out of Egypt and into the land of Canaan to displace a depraved people. The location of the nation of Israel was advantageous to the Word of God being spread throughout the

Mesopotamian region because it was at the center of the Fertile Crescent trade route. Men coming from both east and west would have to pass through and learn of these "peculiar" people who worshiped a God they couldn't see.

The only problem was that these people of God started imitating the ways of other nations and failed to be the light God intended. He scattered them in judgment and then brought back some of them in preparation for the coming of Jesus. A most interesting Biblical passage is found in Galatians, where Paul says,

> But when the fullness of the time came, God sent forth His Son, born of a woman, born under the Law.[3]

What does the fullness of the time mean? Why was this the most appropriate time for Jesus to appear?

God apparently arranged three world situations to prepare for the coming of Jesus. First, judgment of His own people, the Jews, dispersed those people throughout the known world. In almost every place there was a synagogue where faithful Jews proclaimed prophecies of the coming Messiah. When the Messiah came and gave a commission to His church to spread the gospel to the whole world, those synagogues provided a starting place for the proclamation.

Second, approximately three hundred years prior to Jesus' birth, a man known as Alexander the Great conquered most of the Mediterranean and Asian world. The culture he spread included a language, Greek, which became a second language for most people. This demolished the language barrier and men could understand the gospel message. Most of the New Testament originally was written in Greek.

Third, an empire emerged that united the known world politically. The Romans, seeking their own glory, became unwitting allies of God's purposes. Their military might enforced a peace throughout the empire. They also were prodigious road builders. A network of roads extended from Rome to almost every corner of its domain. The peaceful condition combined with the roadway system to make the spreading of the gospel significantly easier than it would have been in a fragmented world.

These three factors taken together—the Jewish dispersion, the Greek language, and the Roman peace and roads—constitute the fullness of the time in Galatians. They are a testimony to God's ability to accomplish His purposes in the world.

With the coming of the gospel, God moved the primary historical scene to Europe (through Greece and Rome), which He then employed as the Continent of Development.

No one can confuse Europe with Asia. Its geographic individuality is evident. The most obvious contrast is its size, followed closely by its barriers. Europe is much smaller than Asia, and no mountain range approaches the Himalayas in size. Europe's smallness and its lack of great barriers made it perfect for the interaction of different types of people, the opposite of God's purposes in Asia. Further, because of its smallness, no one was far from the sea. These factors worked together to promote greater trade, both in commerce and ideas.

The gospel got its greatest foothold in Europe, which was the first continent to be Christianized. Although European Christianity grew increasingly corrupt through the Middle Ages, Europe also was the scene for the restoration of the Christian message through the Reformation, which began in the sixteenth century. This commerce in ideas also formed the basis for the Scientific Revolution of the sixteenth and seventeenth centuries, a revolution founded squarely on a Christian view of the world as the creation of God, intended for men to study, for His glory.

There were, however, limits to the accomplishments in Europe. Belief in the union of church and state remained strong. Whenever the government determined orthodoxy, individual liberty of conscience was stifled. England, geographically separated from the rest of the European continent, was the first nation to become completely Protestant, due largely to its geographic position, safe from the Catholic Church's attempts to return her to the fold militarily. But even in England, citizens had to conform to government-dictated orthodoxy. If Reformation was to be complete, God would have to use another land.

God had hidden such a land ever since the Babel dispersion. Yes, there were inhabitants—people who had crossed from Asia to Alaska and down into the northern and southern continents of the western hemisphere. But they were not a people with an understanding of the gospel, and therefore not in the mainstream of what God was trying to accomplish in the world. They had developed civilizations, but had given themselves over to religious superstitions that included child sacrifices and well-developed methods of torture for their enemies. The New World was a land ripe for the gospel and for the type of government and culture the gospel was to inspire.

South America became home to a non-Reformation influence from Europe. North America, though, became the Continent of Christian Liberty, particularly that portion of North America that ultimately formed the United States.

Set apart from both Europe and Asia by two vast oceans, North America developed with minimal interference from the Old World. The lack of physical barriers—the first major barrier being the Rocky Mountains, approximately two thousand miles to the west—allowed both expansion and the development of a sense of union among the people.

Many of the first settlers, particularly in New England and Pennsylvania, came in search of liberty of conscience for themselves. They also sought to apply Christian principles to all of society, even to their understanding of government. In God's providential workings, the United States performed two specific purposes: to be the first people to unite Christian principles with governmental structure and to serve as a missionary station, sending the gospel to the rest of the world.

God, therefore, has used geographic individuality to carry out His specific purposes in the history of mankind. Whether one looks at Asia, Europe, or North America, one can see His hand in key historical developments and events.

Individuality in the Animal World

Individuality also shows in the creation of animals. Genesis reveals that God made each animal species. There is one phrase that keeps repeating throughout the creation account, applicable both to plants and animals. That phrase is "after their kind." Whenever God made one type of animal and gave it the power to reproduce, it could only reproduce another of its same kind. Right from the beginning, then, God placed limits and stamped each animal with distinctness and uniqueness. There would be no crossover from one type of animal to another, thereby Biblically excluding any evolutionary explanation for the origin and development of life.

But what about the God of variety? Just because He placed limits on species doesn't mean He ceased loving variety. My daughter, when she was younger, was a horse lover and could lecture on the glories of the different breeds of horses. She had no trouble distinguishing among Arabians, Belgians, Appaloosas, and Quarter horses. To me they are simply horses, but to one who studies them, the variety is evident.

The same can be said about any species of animal—cats, dogs, mice, elephants, sea creatures of all types, and birds of every feather. God has established variety within the clearly defined Biblical "kinds."

God's unique gift to animals is the endowment of instinct. Instinct is unlearned behavior that is recognizable and predictable. It also is inherited. The peacock displays its feathers; no one taught it to do so. Spiders spin webs, worms burrow in the ground, predatory animals use the same techniques from one generation to another, and birds build nests—all without real instruction on how to do any of these things. Man has certain unlearned reflex actions, but nothing approaching the complexity of the animal instinct.

There remains the element of purpose. Man uses each "kind" of animal for different, yet definite, purposes. Certain dogs specialize in hunting. Horses, depending on the type, are used either for riding or for heavy work. Bees make honey for human consumption, and cows not only give milk, but are a source of meat. The list could go on, but the undeniable fact remains: the animal world, like the physical world, is imbued with individuality—distinctness, uniqueness, identity, and purpose.

Individuality and Man

> Then God said, "Let Us make man in Our image, according to Our likeness; and let them rule over the fish of the sea and over the birds of the sky and over the

cattle and over all the earth, and over every creeping thing that creeps on the earth." And God created man in His own image, in the image of God He created him; male and female He created them. And God blessed them; and God said to them, "Be fruitful and multiply, and fill the earth, and subdue it; and rule over the fish of the sea and over the birds of the sky, and over every living thing that moves on the earth."[4]

Man was God's crowning achievement in creation. He made a clear demarcation line between man and other created things. Only man was given the image of God. He can think, feel, and choose—the same abilities God possesses. Mankind is set apart as something special. Men are the unique creation of God for a specific purpose, to rule and reign over the rest of His creation and, as other Scriptures reveal, to walk in communion with the Creator.

God not only made man a higher part of creation, but He also gave each person an identity and specific purpose. Both internal and external features manifest this personal individuality.

Externally, it is usually not difficult to tell one person from another (even identical twins have differences). The most obvious distinguishing feature is gender. From the beginning, God created male and female for the propagation of the race. That purpose is easily understood.

Beyond the gender difference, however, are many other differences, with bodily appearance at the top of the list. Hair (color, texture), eyes (color, shape), nose (shape, length), teeth (each dental configuration is individual), skin color, and body build (stocky versus slender) all contribute to the uniqueness of each person.

The external qualities do not end with appearance. As mentioned previously, others had recognized my particular manner of walking. We all have certain mannerisms and gestures that identify us as *us*.

Voices are unique; we can identify people by voice alone, once we know them well enough. Beyond voice recognition by the human ear, though, there is now a scientific method to identify each particular voice. A sound spectrograph records the time, frequency, and intensity of speech-sound waves. These waves are then graphed and compared to other voice graphs (or voiceprints)—each different from the other. What this technology accomplishes is confirmation of the principle of individuality.

Police use fingerprints to identify criminals. The reason? Each individual's set of fingerprints is unique. This is also true of handwriting. Each person's writing is distinctly his own; forgery is not easily learned.

Although externals are important, they are not the essence of individuality. The qualities given by God that truly provide uniqueness are internal.

We know that the image of God mentioned in Gen. 1:26-28 is not something external; it applies to the internal qualities with which God has endowed man. I have mentioned three of these qualities already—man's abilities to think, to feel, and to choose.

Each human being has intelligence. Rational thought is a clear dividing line between man and the rest of creation. Yet the intelligence of each person is unique, both in level and type. For instance, some people can digest complex thought, while others, no matter how hard they may apply themselves, will find a certain limitation on this ability.

Yet just because someone may not be Ph.D. material does not mean he has been shortchanged. There are also different types of intelligence. I am a Ph.D., but have no native ability to fix anything; I always rely on those who have the capacity to understand how an engine works whenever my car gives me trouble. It is conceivable, with a considerable time commitment, that I could do it myself, but it is not the natural bent of my intelligence.

I discovered the same principle when, in high school, I first realized that math did not always mean working with numbers. I had usually received A's in math throughout my first eight years. Then, in ninth grade, I was introduced to algebra. I survived and moved on to geometry. My survival in geometry was shakier, but sufficient to lead me on to a more advanced algebra. One semester and a C– later, I ran into something called a parabola. At that point something seemed to disconnect between my brain and the algebra book, and I quickly dropped the course.

The same thing happened in chemistry my senior year. For the first time in my life I received a D. Officers in the National Honor Society are not supposed to get D's. Although I eventually passed, chemistry did not improve my overall grade average.

This incapacity for math and science provided a challenge for me when, as a Christian school headmaster a decade later, my science teacher quit midyear. No one else was available to teach, so I spent most of my Christmas vacation learning everything I could about physical science. Except for one lab experiment that emptied the school (I'm still not sure exactly what went wrong), the students got what they needed the rest of the year.

Intellectual individuality relates closely to individual God-given talents and abilities. I enjoy reading, researching, writing, and teaching because I have some talent for those activities. For others, reading and research is a bore, writing a virtual impossibility, and public speaking, or teaching, an unspeakable form of torture. My wife used to be the director of an administrative computer center; she has that ability or talent. Yet no one could devise a more vicious form of torture for me. I appreciate her talents and I know God uses them, but I prefer what I do and trust that God can use me as well.

We also are individual in our emotions. Each person has the full gamut of emotions to draw upon, but different ones are dominant, depending on the person. Everyone feels anger, but some are more naturally disposed toward anger. Probably no one has ever gone through life without crying, yet some are naturally more sensitive individuals who will cry over situations that do not affect others the same way.

God uses both types. He wants people to feel righteous anger over issues such as abortion. It is the angry person—as long as the anger is channeled properly and doesn't control one's actions—who may win a great victory on that front. And there is always a need for sensitive people to accomplish God's will. The sensitive person, however, needs to be balanced; sensitivity must not overrule reason.

Another aspect of God's image in man is the power of choice, or free will. We all must respond to God on an individual basis; no one gets saved as part of a group. Although God desires each person to submit to Him, such submission must be the result of willingness by the individual. Free will takes on even greater significance when we turn to other principles later in the book.

Probably the most important individual characteristic given to man is his spirit. That also is part of the image of God. For the present, we inhabit what the apostle Paul calls "earthly vessels."[5] It is through the external qualities mentioned previously that we identify one another. There is, however, a deeper identification, an identification of spirit. In heaven, even before we receive our resurrection bodies, we still will know each other because our spirits will be recognizable.

The external and internal characteristics can be summarized as follows:

INTERNAL	EXTERNAL
Intelligence	Appearance
Talents & Abilities	Gestures
Emotions	Mannerisms
Free Will	Voice
Spirit	Fingerprints

In the New Testament, no greater testimony to the principle of individuality can be found than the passage in I Corinthians that describes the Body of Christ:

> For the body is not one member, but many. If the foot should say, "Because I am not a hand, I am not a part of the body," it is not for this reason any the less a part of the body. And if the ear should say, "Because I am not an eye, I am not a part of the body," it is not for this reason any the less a part of the body. If the whole body were an eye, where would the hearing be? If the whole were hearing, where would the sense of smell be? But now God has placed the members, each one of them, in the body, just as He desired.[6]

This is a clear declaration that we all perform different functions or purposes, and that God decides each purpose. Paul continues,

> And the eye cannot say to the hand, "I have no need of you"; or again the head to the feet, "I have no need of you." On the contrary, it is much truer that the members of the body which seem to be weaker are neces-

sary; and those members of the body, which we deem less honorable, on these we bestow more abundant honor, and our unseemly members come to have more abundant seemliness, whereas our seemly members have no need of it. But God has so composed the body, giving more abundant honor to that member which lacked, that there should be no division in the body, but that the members should have the same care for one another.[7]

This is an affirmation that no matter what gifts God has given to an individual, they are to be considered worthwhile because God is the giver. The reason for the differing gifts and unique functions is that God wanted it that way. Through the differences He wants mutual respect and appreciation to grow. Although certain members of the body—and their gifts—may not appear very glamorous, the body will not perform properly without them.

Paul concludes the chapter with a catalog of the distinct ministries God has ordained in the church:

Now you are Christ's body, and individually members of it. And God has appointed in the church, first apostles, second prophets, third teachers, then miracles, then gifts of healings, helps, administrations, various kinds of tongues. All are not apostles, are they? All are not prophets, are they? All are not teachers, are they? All are not workers of miracles, are they? All do not have gifts of healings, do they? All do not speak with tongues, do they? All do not interpret, do they?[8]

While there may be times that each person will teach, bring healing, or be involved in administration, others have specific ministries in these areas. They have individual purposes carved out for them by God. There are enough ministries to go around; no one is left out of God's purposes.

Individuality also shows through the Biblical writers. There is no mistaking Paul for John. Paul is scholarly and uses complex sentence structure, while John employs a simple, even repetitive, approach. God used their unique personalities and abilities to deliver His message.

The four gospels bear the stamp of the individuality of each writer. Matthew's purpose was to convince the Jews that Jesus was the Messiah. His gospel, written for the Jews, constantly refers to the Old Testament prophecies and shows how Jesus fulfilled each one. Mark, according to most commentators, wrote his gospel for Peter, a man of action. That quality is seen throughout Mark. Action is the key to the gospel; the word "immediately" occurs ten times in the first chapter alone, each time referring to an action taken either by Jesus or someone else. Its emphasis on action makes Mark a shorter gospel, less focused on everything Jesus said.

The opposite is true of Luke, which is the most detailed accounting of Jesus' life and ministry. Luke "investigated everything carefully from the beginning" so that his reader "might know the exact truth about the things you have been taught."[9] John, meanwhile, concentrates on the philosophical discourses of Jesus; there are speeches in John that cannot be found in any of the other gospels. In all, the four gospels present a well-rounded picture of the life and message of Jesus, employing the distinctive qualities of four individuals who became His disciples.

Individuality in God

Why is there so much individuality in the world, whether one looks at the physical, animal, or human level? The answer comes back again to God the Source.

Individuality reigns in the Godhead, so naturally His creation would express what is present in God. The Christian concept of God comprises three distinct persons: Father, Son, and Holy Spirit. They are distinct, as shown by the baptism of Jesus by John the Baptist. When Jesus submitted to John's baptism, a voice spoke from heaven declaring Him to be "My beloved Son, in whom I am well-pleased." Simultaneously, the Bible records that the Holy Spirit descended upon Jesus in the form of a dove. All three persons of the Godhead were involved and they were unique.[10]

It is easy to recognize the distinct purposes of each member of the Godhead. Scripture pictures God the Father as the Creator—He is the focus of the Old Testament. Jesus, the Son, is the Redeemer—His death and resurrection form the centerpiece of the gospels. The Father sends the Holy Spirit to give believers power to become witnesses to the truth.[11] He is the active agent in the world today, in perfect unity with the Father and the Son.

Consequently, the world and all it contains are simply a reflection of the nature of God. The uniqueness, distinctness, identity, and purpose we see around us can first be found in Him. We know we are on solid Biblical ground when we speak of a principle of individuality because it is so evident in God Himself.

Individuality and Civil Government

Recognition of the uniqueness and purpose of each individual should be a requisite for civil government. Throughout history, though, recognition of this principle has been spotty at best; the opposite has been the norm.

People who understand Biblical individuality should acknowledge both the importance of the individual and the need for civil government to safeguard this special creation of God. Government should exist for the individual, not the individual for government. Unfortunately, the latter has been true most of the time.

Once men forgot the true knowledge of God and degenerated into polytheistic superstition, the civil government became a substitute god. In all the early Mesopotamian civilizations and in Egypt, the individual was considered the servant of the state. The situation did not improve in ancient Greece and Rome. In the political theories of Plato and Aristotle, and in the actual practice of the Greek city-states, the individual had importance only if he made a significant contribution to his city. Rome developed a system of civil law that appeared to safeguard certain "rights," but it considered the government, not a creator, to be the grantor. If the government gives rights, it can take them away.

Both Greece and Rome displayed callousness toward the individual in another way—in their practice of abortion and infanticide. Abortion was commonplace and infanticide excused as long as the newborn did not have a name. The baby, without a name, was not considered a real person.

Christianity stood against this practice. A mid-second-century document called the *Didache*, or *The Teaching of the Twelve Apostles*, plainly declared, "You shall not procure an abortion or kill the newborn child."[12] Although the Christian message suffered corruption during the Middle Ages, basic respect for the individual remained intact. The Reformation continued the early abortion beliefs, and a Christian framework of thinking dominated until the onset of evolutionary philosophy.

The United States, in its founding document, the Declaration of Independence, declared God to be the Creator of man and the giver of man's rights to life (the value of the individual made in the image of God), liberty (self-government—see the next chapter), and the pursuit of happiness (happiness defined in that day as the will of God for each individual, not as "do your own thing"). The type of government set up by the Constitution respected the individual and acknowledged certain guarantees for his protection. After the abolition of slavery in the mid-nineteenth century, it appeared that the principle of individuality was secure. But things changed.

The theory of evolution gained wide acceptance after the Civil War. By the end of the nineteenth century, the new "science" had won the day and its champions applied its biological assumptions to society.

How has evolutionary theory altered the way in which we view man? No longer is man the creation of God—unique, distinct, and clearly identified as made in God's image for a specific purpose. Evolutionary proponents deny his unique position in creation. Man is simply a higher form of animal. Those who take this philosophy to its logical conclusion see man as little more than a mass of chemicals, lacking a spirit. Viewed in this manner, man has no more significance than a grain of sand. Consequently, it is not hard to take the step from man as a grain of sand to unborn man as a mass of tissue, easily aborted if inconvenient.

The belief that man is no more than a higher form of animal has birthed destructive educational-psychological theories. Behavioral psychology began to study and treat man as an animal. External stimuli were to produce certain responses. Perhaps, these theorists reasoned, we can produce the type of society "we" want by experimenting on man.

This philosophy obliterated the Biblical picture of man as made in the image of God, but in particular it omitted man's free will, describing him instead as a bio-

51

logical organism conditioned to respond in prescribed ways. Although it is difficult to find pure behaviorists these days, the philosophy still merges with others to create a humanistic, man-centered emphasis.

Evolutionary philosophy also produced philosophical pragmatism, which simply means that whatever works is true. Everything evolves; truth must evolve also. This bred moral relativism, which soon dominated the field of law and subsequently affected how government operates. Principle was lost; expediency became the watchword. President Franklin D. Roosevelt built his New Deal program in the 1930s on political pragmatism—do whatever works. In the name of protecting the rights of individuals, he began a trend toward ever-more-intrusive civil government that has as its goal the absolute conformity of each individual to the government's idea of what is good.

We have never heard more about individual rights, yet never have individual liberties been so threatened. American government decrees what man's rights are; God is no longer consulted. We are coming dangerously close to man's usual mode of government, in which the individual exists for the state.

Individuality must be recovered. As stated at the beginning of this chapter, it is the cornerstone for all the other principles. If individuality is lost, the other principles have no basis. That is precisely what we are witnessing in American government and society today—the erosion of every Biblical principle. We must return to God the Source.

CHAPTER 3

SELF-GOVERNMENT: MATURITY AND LIBERTY

Hugo Grotius (1583-1645) was a Dutch lawyer, scholar, theologian, and author. His most famous work, *The Law of War and Peace*, made him famous as the foremost authority on the law of nations. One quote attributed to Grotius is one of the most insightful (and Biblical) statements on government I have ever read:

> He knows not how to rule a kingdom, that cannot manage a province; nor can he wield a province, that cannot order a city; nor he order a city, that knows not how to regulate a village; nor he a village, that cannot guide a family; nor can that man govern well a family that knows not how to govern himself; neither can any govern himself unless his reason be lord, will and appetite her vassals; nor can reason rule unless herself be ruled by God, and be obedient to Him.[1]

Grotius is saying that men cannot manage something large if they already are having trouble with something small. He ultimately brings it down to the control of oneself under God. This insight by Grotius agrees with a passage of Scripture in I Timothy dealing with leadership in the church:

> An overseer, then, must be above reproach, the husband of one wife, temperate, prudent, respectable, hospitable, able to teach, not addicted to wine or pugnacious, but gentle, uncontentious, free from the love of money. He must be one who manages his own household well, keeping his children under control with all dignity (but if a man does not know how to manage his own household, how will he take care of the church of God?).[2]

In other words, if the individual is out of control, it will adversely affect his ability to govern anything else. Both the Grotian quote and the Biblical passage focus on the importance of self-government.

Individual Governors

A proper understanding of self-government first requires a comprehension of government, which is simply control and direction. When something is controlled, it is restrained by force. When it is directed, it is led on the right course. Consequently, *self*-government is the ability to restrain oneself and follow a right course without someone else always overseeing and directing one's life. In function, self-government is synonymous with maturity.

Although the intent of this book is to apply these principles to civil government, it is important to realize that civil government is only one type of government. There are other governments: family, church, and various businesses and organizations. Wherever individuals get together to accomplish a purpose, one finds government. Yet the fundamental government is that of the self, because the level of self-government will determine how well groups of people govern themselves.

All government begins with the individual. Each person is a governor charged by God with the responsibility of governing himself properly, according to His Word. Anytime the Bible gives a command, the assumption is that people have the responsibility, and the ability, to obey. God told Adam,

> From any tree of the garden you may eat freely; but from the tree of the knowledge of good and evil you shall not eat, for in the day that you eat from it you shall surely die.[3]

The term "self-government" is not used in this passage, but the intent is the same. God desired Adam to control and direct his life properly, by following the commands given him. When Adam and Eve disobeyed one of God's commandments, they departed from Biblical self-government. Lack of self-government has another name used throughout the Bible—sin.

In Proverbs, the book of sound advice, men are reminded:

> He who is slow to anger is better than the mighty, and he who rules his spirit, than he who captures a city.[4]

This is reminiscent of the Grotian quote and the I Timothy passage. From God's perspective, a man who is in control of himself is worthy of greater honor than a military conqueror.

There have been many "great" men in history, at least by standards other than God's. Perhaps no one illustrates this proverb better than Alexander the Great, who conquered most of the known world from 336-323 B.C. His military genius and the speed with which he overran other empires astounded the world. He came to believe in his own divinity and demanded that the cities under his control declare him a god. Yet shortly after his subjects agreed to this demand, he died of the effects of gluttony and drunkenness. He was only thirty-three years old. Alexander the Great captured cities, but did not rule his own spirit.

The New Testament speaks of self-government when it uses the word "self-control." Since government is control, self-control is merely a synonym for self-government. When the Apostle Paul had the opportunity to explain the gospel to the Roman Procurator Felix, we are told:

> As he was discussing righteousness, **self-control** and the judgment to come, Felix became frightened and said, "Go away for the present, and when I find time, I will summon you."[5]

Felix didn't like Paul's message; it called for self-government, but he was not willing to govern himself according to God's laws.

When Paul wrote to the Corinthians, he again emphasized the need for self-government:

> Do you not know that those who run in a race all run, but only one receives the prize? Run in such a way that you may win. And everyone who competes in the games exercises **self-control** in all things. They then do it to receive a perishable wreath, but we an imperishable.[6]

The prize of eternal life depends on self-government. The Apostle Peter echoes this in his catalogue of qualities that should be evident in a Christian life. He instructs believers to add self-control to their other character traits, and tells them, "If these qualities are yours and are increasing, they render you neither useless nor unfruitful in the true knowledge of our Lord Jesus Christ."[7]

Paul's listing of the fruit of the Spirit in Galatians includes self-control. If self-government is not demonstrated in a person's life, one can question whether that person is "in" the Spirit, for as Paul goes on to say,

> Now those who belong to Christ Jesus have crucified the flesh with its passions and desires. If we live by the Spirit, let us also walk by the Spirit.[8]

Self-control, or self-government, is an inescapable Biblical doctrine.

External and Internal Self-Government

Self-government is first internal, then external. It is the external, however, that people notice. We look at a person's actions to determine if he is in control of himself. A man who sticks all his bills in a drawer and tries to ignore them is not self-governed in his financial life. A college student who rarely shows up for class is not governing his time properly or taking his responsibilities seriously. An employee who will not do his work without constant supervision exhibits a lack of self-government. I could multiply examples.

One's appearance also gives clues to the level of self-government. A person who never grooms properly or who always dresses sloppily is not governing his external appearance. The student who slouches in his seat, keeps his hat on in the classroom (all the better for disguising the desire to sleep), and does not take notes sends a signal to his teacher that he is not really interested in educational pursuits. Although external appearance is not the whole story, it does leave an impression that is difficult to overcome.

Probably a key area of external self-government is what comes out of one's mouth. A person's speech can cause considerable damage. Paul remarks,

> Let no unwholesome word proceed from your mouth, but only such a word as is good for edification according to the need of the moment, that it may give grace to those who hear.[9]

The word translated "unwholesome" in the New American Standard Bible has a deeper meaning in the original Greek. It [sapros] means "rotten; putrid; worthless," and provides a much stronger image than the one supplied simply by the word "unwholesome."[10]

As if Paul's exhortation were not enough, the Scripture offers a blistering passage in the book of James:

> For we all stumble in many ways. If any one does not stumble in what he says, he is a perfect man, able to bridle the whole body as well.... Behold, the ships also, though they are so great and are driven by strong winds, are still directed by a very small rudder, wherever the inclination of the pilot desires. So also the tongue is a small part of the body, and yet it boasts of great things. Behold, how great a forest is set aflame by such a small fire! And the tongue is a fire, the very world of iniquity; the tongue is set among our members as that which defiles the entire body, and sets on fire the course of our life, and is set on fire by hell.... No one can tame the tongue; it is a restless evil and full of deadly poison. With it we bless our Lord and Father; and with it we curse men, who have been made in the likeness of God; from the same mouth come both blessing and cursing. My brethren, these things ought not to be this way.[11]

James makes taming the tongue sound impossible, but he is emphasizing *external* efforts to govern one's speech. All such efforts are ultimately doomed to failure because there is an internal aspect that must first be self-governed under God before any external self-government will be effective.

Paul warns both the Galatian and Colossian Christians against an emphasis on externals. They were turning back to the Jewish Law, believing that obedience to a list of rules would secure their salvation. To the Galatians he exclaimed,

> You foolish Galatians, who has bewitched you, before whose eyes Jesus Christ was publicly portrayed as crucified? This is the only thing I want to find out from you: Did you receive the Spirit by the works of the Law, or by hearing with faith? Are you so foolish? Having begun by the Spirit, are you now being perfected by the flesh?[12]

And again:

> It was for freedom that Christ set us free; therefore keep standing firm and do not be subject again to a yoke of slavery.... You have been severed from Christ, you who are seeking to be justified by law; you have fallen from grace.[13]

To the Colossians, Paul is quite explicit:

> Therefore let no one act as your judge in regard to food or drink or in respect to a festival or a new moon or a Sabbath day—things which are a mere shadow of what is to come; but the substance belongs to Christ.... If you have died with Christ to the elementary principles of the world, why, as if you were living in the world, do you submit yourself to decrees, such as, "Do

not handle, do not taste, do not touch!" (which all refer to things destined to perish with the using) in accordance with the commandments and teachings of men? These are matters which have, to be sure, the appearance of wisdom in self-made religion and self-abasement and severe treatment of the body, but are of no value against fleshly indulgence.[14]

Self-made religion and self-abasement, both of which concentrate on external control, are different from self-government. One achieves true self-government only when one allows God to fill the thoughts, attitudes, motives, and emotions. The Scripture gives specific instruction in each of these internal areas.

Biblical self-government begins with the mind. It must be made new in Christ and be placed into subjection to His mind. As Paul says in Romans,

And do not be conformed to this world, but be transformed by the renewing of your mind, that you may prove what the will of God is, that which is good and acceptable and perfect.[15]

Some churches believe that being conformed to this world relates to the type of clothing a person wears, whether jewelry is part of one's apparel, or if one's entertainment includes movies. While there may be good reasons not to wear certain types of clothing and to avoid certain movies, these are externals. Renewal of the mind must come first. A person with a renewed mind might not go see a certain movie, but the reason will come from within, from a deep conviction that it dishonors God. All too often, the list of rules becomes paramount, and the spirit behind the rules is lost.

The renewal of the mind is continuous. It is not a one-time occurrence. A Christian never reaches a point where he can say that the renewal has been completed; God always has more light to shine on our lives. The more renewed a person becomes, the less he will be conformed to the world.

The renewal of the mind is dependent upon what enters the mind. Paul instructs the Corinthians:

> We are destroying speculations and every lofty thing raised up against the knowledge of God, and we are taking every thought captive to the obedience of Christ.[16]

Taking every thought captive to the obedience of Christ means that His thoughts must dominate; one must exclude anything contrary to His ways. The old saying is still true: "You can't stop a bird from flying over your head, but you can keep him from building a nest in your hair." The application to one's thoughts should be obvious: sinful thoughts may pass through the mind, but they don't need to be given a dwelling place. The first step in self-government occurs when the thought life is subject to the Holy Spirit.

A second area for internal self-government is attitudes. When Jesus rebuked the Pharisees in Matthew 12, He focused on their attitude, and at the same time commented eloquently on the relationship between internal and external:

> You brood of vipers, how can you, being evil, speak what is good? For the mouth speaks out of that which fills the heart. The good man out of his good treasure brings forth what is good; and the evil man out of his evil treasure brings forth what is evil. And I say to you, that every careless word that men shall speak, they shall render account for it in the day of judgment. For

by your words you shall be justified, and by your words you shall be condemned.[17]

What filled the hearts of the Pharisees? A careful reading of Jesus' other denunciations suggests that they were full of pride because of their exalted position in society. They also were jealous of Jesus because He taught with authority and God honored His words with healings and other miracles. Even the report of the raising of Lazarus from the dead did not convince them to fall down and worship, but instead encouraged them to seek a way to kill this Teacher who was exposing their false leadership. Their attitude of pride and envy kept them from recognizing the hand of God. This is why Jesus pointedly remarked that the mouth speaks out of that which fills the heart.

The final verse in the passage makes it seem that a man will be judged by words alone—an external manifestation. But, in context, words are merely the outgrowth of what is in the heart. If internal attitudes are not self-governed, external words also are out of control. This hearkens back to the verses about the tongue in James. The external tongue is the cause of so many problems because men do not have internal self-government.

The writer of Hebrews also deals with an attitude:

Pursue after peace with all men, and after the sanctification without which no one will see the Lord. See to it that no one comes short of the grace of God; that no root of bitterness springing up cause trouble, and by it many be defiled.[18]

There are three attitudes described here: the pursuit of peace with all men, the desire for sanctification, and a root of bitterness. The first is a heart attitude that seeks to work in harmony with other people; the opposite is the person who always seems to live for controversy. The second is a hunger to reach the fullness of the Christian life; this Scripture even declares that without this hunger there is no guarantee that a person will be in God's kingdom.

The third attitude is a source of all kinds of heartache. The Greek word translated as bitterness [pikria] is used in other New Testament passages. In Acts 8, Simon the Sorcerer sought to buy the ability to bestow the Holy Spirit upon people. Peter accused him of being bound by bitterness and demanded that he repent and receive forgiveness. In Romans 3, Paul uses the word in his description of men who refuse to follow God. And in Ephesians 4, the word is connected with grieving away the Holy Spirit. Bitterness is a serious attitude problem. Hebrews 12 adds the understanding that bitterness can be a "root" and that it can defile many.

A root is the part of the plant that goes deeply into the soil and forms the anchor for the entire plant. Similarly, someone who has a root of bitterness is firmly anchored in that attitude. The root of a plant is the source of sustenance that permits the plant to bring forth fruit. The root of bitterness also leads to the production of fruit; the writer of Hebrews says this fruit is the defilement of many, meaning this bitterness spreads to other people, ruining their attitudes also. Lack of self-government allows bitterness to grow.

The attitude of a person self-governed under God is described by Paul in Philippians:

> Have this attitude in yourselves which was also in Christ Jesus, who, although He existed in the form of God, did not regard equality with God a thing to be grasped, but emptied Himself, taking the form of a bondservant, and being made in the likeness of men. And being found in appearance as a man, He humbled

Himself by becoming obedient to the point of death, even death on a cross.[19]

Jesus is the model. Believers are to take on His mind *and* His attitude. If thoughts and attitudes are subject to His will, self-government has a fertile field in which to grow.

God is interested in motives as well. A verse in the book of Hebrews is foundational to this understanding:

> For the word of God is living and active and sharper than any two-edged sword, and piercing as far as the division of soul and spirit, of both joints and marrow, and able to judge the thoughts and intentions of the heart.[20]

The intentions of the heart are a man's motives—*why* he does the things he does. A person can do all the "right" things for all the wrong reasons. As Jesus noted in the Sermon on the Mount,

> Beware of practicing your righteousness before men to be noticed by them; otherwise you have no reward with your Father who is in heaven. When therefore you give alms, do not sound the trumpet before you, as the hypocrites do in the synagogues and in the streets, that they may be honored by men.... And when you pray, you are not to be as the hypocrites; for they love to stand and pray in the synagogues and on the street corners, in order to be seen by men.... And whenever you fast, do not put on a gloomy face as the hypocrites do; for they neglect their appearance in order to be seen fasting by men.[21]

According to this passage, having a wrong motive in doing good deeds is hypocrisy.

Charles G. Finney, who possibly was the most effective evangelist of nineteenth-century America, was adept at highlighting people's motives. His goal was to break down every defense man raises against God's truth. As a result, he could be quite piercing in his remarks. He was particularly effective when preaching on the difference between "true saints" and "deceived persons."[22]

Both agree on the importance of a moral life, yet the true saint, says Finney, "leads a moral life from love to holiness;... The true saint loves it [the moral life] as an end." The deceived person simply "uses morality as a means to an end, his own happiness." He wants to be moral, but from selfish considerations.

On prayer, Finney states, "The true saint loves to pray; the other prays because he hopes to derive some benefit to himself from praying." The true saint expects benefit from prayer, but "that is not his leading motive. The other prays from no other motive."

The deceived person may be zealous in working for God, but only "for the sake of having his own salvation more assured, and because he is afraid of going to hell if he does not work for the Lord, or to quiet his conscience, and not because he loves religion for its own sake." "Who ever doubted," Finney continues, "that a person might give his money to the Bible Society, or the Missionary Society, from selfish motives alone, to procure happiness, or applause, or obtain the favor of God?" By the time Finney finished preaching, each person would be questioning his own motives. Yet this is no less than what Jesus taught in the Sermon on the Mount.

A truly self-governed motive, then, is to do all things out of love for God, and not for selfish purposes. When a person's motive is no longer dominated by selfishness, his external actions will be genuine, and not hypocritical.

The final area of concern for internal self-government is the emotions. This can be one of the hardest areas, primarily because the will cannot directly control the emotions. It is nearly impossible to think, "I am now going to feel this emotion" and achieve the desired feeling immediately, particularly if the opposite emotion already has come to the forefront. One cannot help feeling angered at the sight of a friend being brutally beaten. The anger arises even without thinking. When a loved one dies, grief is natural, and it is quite difficult to govern that spontaneous feeling. Yet governed it must be.

Sometimes it is tempting to wish God had not given these emotions; life might be easier without them. Yet emotions are part of the image of God. They should be considered helpful, not detrimental. Righteous anger, as stated in the last chapter, can lead to effective action. Grief can be a friend as individuals learn to feel the way God feels about sin and death; neither sin nor death was a part of His original plan. And who would want to live a life that didn't include the feeling of joy?

Self-government of the emotions merely means that feelings will not dictate actions or speech. As Paul warns in Ephesians,

> Be angry, and yet do not sin; do not let the sun go down on your anger, and do not give the devil an opportunity.[23]

There is room for anger without sin. But dwelling on anger will lead to sin. Again, it is similar to the idea that one does not let a bird build a nest in one's hair. The emotion is present, but if that emotion leads to an action, righteousness usually is sacrificed; actions must be based upon Biblical reasoning, not upon an outburst of emotion.

The internal and external spheres of self-government can be summarized as follows:

INTERNAL	EXTERNAL
Thoughts Attitudes Motives Emotions	Actions Appearance Speech

The external is dependent on the internal. The internal is the cause; the external is the effect.

How is internal self-government possible? Government of the thoughts, attitudes, motives, and emotions may seem too difficult a task. It is—if done with gritted teeth and an unregenerate heart. It can be accomplished only through cooperation with the Spirit of God. Paul hints at the solution in his first letter to the Corinthians:

> But by the grace of God I am what I am, and His grace toward me did not prove vain; but I labored even more than all of them [other apostles], yet not I, but the grace of God with me.[24]

He gives a fuller explanation in his letter to the Philippians:

> So then, my beloved, just as you have always obeyed, not as in my presence only, but now much more in my absence, work out your salvation with fear and trembling; for it is God who is at work in you, both to will and to work for His good pleasure.[25]

The Christian life is man's willingness to obey God and God's power for man to carry out what he [man] wills. It is not all man; neither is it all God. It is God and man working together. It can be no less, because God chose to make man in His image, with a free will. Perhaps the writer to the Hebrews sums it up best:

> Now the God of peace, who brought up from the dead the great Shepherd of the sheep through the blood of the eternal covenant, even Jesus our Lord, **equip you** in every good thing to do His will, working in us that which is pleasing in His sight, through Jesus Christ.[26]

God equips; man uses the equipment. Self-government is accomplished.

An External Governor

The kindergartner walked tentatively into the immense (or so it seemed to him) room. Rows and rows of tables and chairs filled his vision. He wasn't quite sure what he was supposed to do or where he should go. To put it bluntly, he wasn't even sure why he was there. He had spent all his life at home and now he was embarking on an adventure, although he wasn't certain it would be an adventure to his liking. What to do? Where to go?

Then, in the midst of his confusion, a smiling woman suddenly popped into view. Her voice was calm and cheerful. She introduced herself as his teacher, told him where to put his things, and showed him where to sit. As the day progressed, she gave more instructions. Later she lined him up with his classmates and led him down a long hall into an even larger room where he was delighted to find lunch prepared for him. At the end of the day he again joined a line, and soon was picked up by mom. He had survived.

The kindergartner in this scenario would have been lost without someone to control and direct his day. Children are not prepared at age five to make all the decisions necessary for success in a foreign place. Even in a familiar home setting, parents must remind a five-year-old to brush his teeth, make his bed, and pick up toys. Lack of maturity, or self-government, requires someone to tell him what to do. He would be lost without an external governor.

A high school senior, however, has developed a certain level of maturity. No one expects to line up seniors for lunch. They may even be free at lunchtime to hop into their cars (a certain level of maturity is essential to earn a driver's license) and go to a restaurant, trusted by school authorities to return in time for the next class. In short, a high school senior is not treated the same as a kindergartner. We recognize that a natural growth in self-government has taken place. Less external authority is needed to keep the senior under control and pointed in the right direction. At least, that is the hope.

As children grow, they must be given more opportunities to learn self-government. Mom and Dad are not always going to be around to oversee every decision. This is as it should be because it is consistent with the image of God placed within each person. No one can come to Him as part of a group or by another's decision. Salvation is a personal decision to deny oneself and take up the cross daily. As self-government under God grows, an individual can handle more responsibilities.

Again the Grotius quote at the beginning of this chapter is instructive: if a man is governed by God, he is ready to govern a family; if he handles the family well, perhaps he can take greater governmental responsibilities, whether in civil government or in another type of organization; and if he handles himself honorably in those responsibilities, additional ones may await him.

But what is to be done with those individuals who never seem to attain maturity? The principle of self-government teaches that if a person does not reach a sufficient level of self-government, it will be essential for him to have an external governor. Control from outside the individual is imperative when that individual refuses to be self-governing. The degree of self-government will determine the amount of oversight and number of rules a person must have.

As a college professor, I look at the students in my classes and see different levels of self-government. The highest level is the student who not only completes the requirements on time and to the best of his ability, but who sometimes turns assignments in early. This is the student who has learned a high degree of self-government. Of course, I see only the external; perhaps wrong motives push such a student. If so, the basic selfishness at the root of this diligence eventually will manifest itself. Yet, as a professor, I can at least appreciate the industry he displays.

At the other end of the spectrum is the student who never turns in anything on time and neglects to study for my essay exams (the only kind worth giving, but that's another book). Even if this student has made a commitment to Christ, there is a low level of self-government and an urgent need for the renewal of the mind mentioned in Romans 12. I then must become an external governor, in the hope that my control and direction will keep the student governed. This is not easy. The goal is to lead the student away from dependence on a higher human authority into a dependence on God that will express itself in Biblical self-government.

Self-Government in the History of the Church

Although self-government begins with the individual, its application is universal. Each family is a self-governing unit. Each business, organization, or club is self-governing. The same is true for local communities, regional communities (states), and even entire countries. We will turn to self-government in civil government in the next section of this chapter, but it is useful to look first at the history of self-government in the church, since much history involves the intertwining of church and state.

When Jesus ascended and God poured out the Holy Spirit on the day of Pentecost, the church was born. Jesus left no hierarchical structure. He had some apostles as spokesmen, but He gave no blueprint for a worldwide organization. I believe this is because He didn't want a worldwide church government.

The testimony of the New Testament is that each church was a local self-governing body. Paul writes to the church at Philippi, the church at Corinth, the church at Rome, all identified by their locales. Although he was an apostle and carried apostolic authority, he could not be in all these places at once. Local church leadership was selected, and the distinct bodies of Christ in each locality governed their own affairs. Although they were part of a universal church in the Spirit, governmentally they were independent.

The New Testament gives only one instance of an assembled council of church leaders (Acts 15). A controversy had arisen over whether Gentile believers should obey Jewish rituals. Yet the apostles residing in Jerusalem did not decree this council; it was a decision by the church at Antioch to send Paul, Barnabas, and others to Jerusalem to receive the benefit of the apostles' spiritual wisdom and maturity. It was a voluntary council. The council's resolutions did not carry the penalty of excommunication or any other show of force if the brethren at Antioch disagreed with the conclusions reached. No great hierarchy existed.

But the situation altered in the next few centuries. Slowly, almost imperceptibly at first, leaders arose to take more extensive authority. Bishops considered themselves spiritual authorities over several churches. Self-government began to erode. Eventually, the church established a system that included not only bishops, but archbishops, cardinals, and a pope. The office of the pope in the Middle Ages became so powerful that anyone in this office became the vicar of Christ on earth, a man with astounding spiritual authority over all the individual churches on the European continent.

This system destroyed God's plan for individual self-governing churches. The church suffered a tremendous spiritual decline because of this manmade hierarchy. The decline set in because the hierarchy went against a spiritual truth—the principle of self-government.

Whenever an organizational hierarchy is set up, authorities at the top make all the important decisions. Those decisions are then passed on through a multitude of levels of authority to those at the bottom. If the doctrinal pronouncement or policy decision from the top is unscriptural, error enters the entire system.

Local self-governing churches would avoid this automatic transmission of error. If one church went into doctrinal error, that error would affect other churches only if they voluntarily chose the same path. Even if many churches departed into heresy, a faithful remnant would maintain the Biblical standard. In a top-heavy hierarchy, no faithful remnant is allowed to survive.

The history of man's organizational church in the Middle Ages, especially toward the end of the period, after the hierarchy hardened into an inflexible form, is full of instances of outright persecution for those who sought to reform the system. The church declared Oxford scholar John Wycliffe (1320-1384) a heretic because he denied the pope's authority, and because he translated the Bible into the language of the English people. Although he did not suffer martyrdom, a later church council dug up his bones and burned them to confirm his "heresy." John Huss, a Czech reformer, was burned at the stake in 1415 for following Wycliffe's ideas.

The Inquisition was set up in the thirteenth century to root out heresies. Inquisition trials operated on the premise that the suspects were guilty and had to prove themselves innocent. If the accused could not prove their innocence and they remained "obstinate," they could suffer imprisonment, torture, or death. Superficially, this inquisitional system was supposed to protect orthodoxy; in reality, it was merely a way to protect the hierarchy— its reputation and its authority.

A second problem with a hierarchy is that it makes everything impersonal. First-century Christians experienced the risen Christ; the Holy Spirit operated in their lives to free them from sinful habit patterns, heal diseases, and perform miracles. The elders and deacons were people they knew. They worshiped with them, prayed with them, and studied the Scriptures together. They answered to these local church authorities, but, ultimately, to God. Being a Christian was a way of life, not an external ritual.

This understanding of the Christian faith changed with the hierarchy. Salvation ceased being a personal relationship with God. Individuals were told that salvation was available only through church membership. Membership was available only through catechism classes and submission to water baptism. Once these external rituals were performed, one could be assured of heaven.

As the hierarchy took dominion over every area of Europe, a person was simply "born" a Christian because he was part of a Christian kingdom. Within the church many layers of officialdom now separated the individual from his God. Prayer to the saints replaced prayer to God the Father. The Christian life became mainly a list of regulations—go to mass, confess to the priest, receive last rites upon one's deathbed. These assured one of salvation.

A third problem with the development of the church hierarchy was that it became united with civil government. In the year 312, Constantine (274-337), a contestant for the throne of the Roman Empire, claimed to see a vision of a cross in the sky and heard a voice say that in this symbol he would conquer. He proclaimed tolerance of Christianity in the region he controlled and went on to defeat other claimants for the title of emperor. In 323, Constantine made Christianity the favored religion of the Empire; one of his successors, Theodosius I (346-395), at the Council of Constantinople in 381, made Christianity the sole official religion of the Empire.

On the surface, the end of persecution and acceptance of the Christian faith by the civil government appeared to be a victory for Christianity. It turned instead into a further deterioration of self-government. Beginning with Constantine, emperors now intruded into church affairs. Civil government interfered with doctrinal issues and often pressured the church to take positions for political reasons. This continued even after the dissolution of the Roman Empire.

A further problem with this unification of church and state was the church's participation in the persecution of those who refused to accept the Christian faith. The government passed edicts forbidding the assembling of heretics and ordering the destruction of pagan temples. While the destruction of pagan temples was an action most Christians could applaud, a dangerous precedent was set, a precedent that made it easier to move into the era of the Inquisition. Christians had changed from being the *persecuted* to being the *persecutors*.

Protest against this system came in the Reformation, initiated in 1517 by a monk named Martin Luther. He had rediscovered personal faith. Luther's revolt soon was picked up by others, and an age of religious wars raged until the Peace of Westphalia in 1648. Many Protestant churches formed, but often they established new hierarchies and self-government remained scarce.

England in the sixteenth century established a national Protestant church, but there was one group of believers that did not agree with the policy that forbade the founding of churches apart from the national establishment. These people became known as Separatists. Government officials persecuted them in the late sixteenth and early seventeenth centuries, so many of them decided to leave their native land.

Their first land of exile was Holland, but eventually they moved to the New World and settled in a town they called Plymouth. American history knows them as the Pilgrims, a people who sought self-government for their churches and for their communities. These Pilgrims gave a new birth to the New Testament concept of individual self-governing churches. The policy they followed in church government also carried over to the civil sphere.

Self-Government and Civil Government

Most ancient peoples knew little about self-government in the political realm. Empires rose and fell. While on the rise, they conquered and subdued others; in decline, the subjugated people broke away, usually to be conquered again by someone else. The only ray of self-government in the era before Christ was in the tiny nation of Israel. Yet even this people turned away from the self-government God decreed for them and greedily latched onto kingship.[27]

When the church developed its hierarchy in the late Roman Empire, it was copying the pyramidal system found within that empire. Emperors gave way to medieval kings. There was a certain amount of self-government within the feudal system, but gradually, as nation-states developed, the idea of the divine right of kings began to dominate political theory. God gave authority directly to certain men, this theory stated, and a king answered to God only. Citizens were merely to obey.

The height of absolutism was during the reign of the French king Louis XIV (1643-1715). His motto, "L'état, c'est moi," [the state, it is I—or I am the state] probably best summarizes his political philosophy. Yet it was during the time of Louis XIV that things began to change, most of all in the New World of America.

When the Pilgrims arrived in America in 1620, their pastor, John Robinson, had to stay behind in Holland with most of the congregation. Yet Robinson had given them instructions on civil government:

> Lastly, whereas you are to become a body politic, administering among yourselves civil government, and are furnished with persons of no special eminence above the rest, from whom you will elect some to the office of government, let your wisdom and godliness appear, not only in choosing such persons as will entirely love and promote the common good, but also in yielding them all due honor and obedience in their lawful administrations; not beholding in them the ordinariness of their persons, but God's ordinance for your good; nor being like the foolish multitude, who honor a gay coat more than either the virtuous mind of the wearer or the glorious ordinance of the Lord. But you know better, and understand that the image of

the Lord's power and authority which the magistrate bears, is honorable, in how humble persons soever. And this duty you can the more willingly perform, because you are at present to have only those for your governors as you yourselves shall choose.[28]

The Pilgrims were to set up their own government, choosing leaders from amongst themselves. Self-government is evident not only in the structure of government they created, but in the type of people they were advised to elect. Robinson urged that only those who were internally self-governed should be chosen to take on the greater responsibility of civil government. The Pilgrims did as he advised and became the model of local self-government for other colonies.

As more American colonies were established, self-government expanded. Royal charters gave permission to set up local assemblies to pass laws. Self-government became the norm for each colony. In fact, self-government became so prominent that the political establishment in England grew alarmed at the possibilities—resulting in what historians usually call the American Revolution. I use the term "American Revolution" simply because it is recognizable to most people. A more accurate title, however, would be "The American War for Independence," or perhaps, "The American War for Continued Self-Government," for self-government was the primary issue.

The British government, by the 1760s, was concerned over the population explosion in the American colonies and the potential for complete independence, thus depriving Britain of a rich source of natural resources and creating a new commercial competitor in the world. These colonies had to be kept under control so they could be managed effectively from across the Atlantic.

The decision to tax and regulate the colonies was entirely inconsistent with the situation. Some of these colonies had been self-governing for more than a century; they were mature politically and did not need oversight. They followed the policies of the British Empire as a whole but had almost total control of their own spheres, electing their own representatives and making their own laws. On occasion, the king might veto a legislature's law, but this was the exception. They were a people experienced in self-government.

When the British Parliament, for the first time in the history of its relationship with the colonies, began passing laws to tax them, an uproar resulted. The colonies lacked a voice in Parliament, thereby making these laws an arbitrary confiscation of personal property. Colonial leaders protested through every legal means offered to them by British precedent.

Representatives met together to discuss the measures and drew up petitions requesting that the British government refrain from invading the realm of local self-government promised by their charters. When the government did not listen on that ground, they switched their argument to a higher plane. Self-government, or liberty, they proclaimed, was a right granted by God, not government. That argument also was ignored.

When the disagreement became an impasse, and more than a year had passed after the first shots were fired, the colonial representatives in Philadelphia reluctantly withdrew all allegiance to the British Empire. "We hold these truths to be self-evident," they declared, "that all men are created equal, that they are endowed by their Creator with certain unalienable Rights." An unalienable [inalienable] right is one that cannot be taken away without one's consent. Such rights were "Life [individuality], Liberty [self-government], and the pursuit of

Happiness [another aspect of self-government under God]." They also appealed "to the Supreme Judge of the World for the rectitude" of their intentions. Further, they stated their "firm reliance on the protection of divine Providence" in the ensuing struggle.[29]

The war ended, ensuring inalienable rights. Self-government, though, on a national scale, was new for these people. They had accomplished it at a regional level, but now encountered problems pulling it together nationally. The Articles of Confederation did not provide a national government strong enough to govern effectively. Yet they were hesitant to create a governmental monstrosity that might wipe out self-government at the state and local levels. The new Constitution of 1787 resolved these concerns. The safeguard for local self-government was the federal system.

The Constitution worked well throughout most of the nineteenth century (the Civil War, of course, being the supreme test of its workability), but by the dawn of the twentieth, foundations had been laid for the erosion of self-government, an erosion manifested first through Progressivism (Woodrow Wilson), then the New Deal (Franklin Roosevelt), and finally, the Great Society (Lyndon Johnson). Government has become more involved with individuals, families, businesses, and even churches. Regulations have increased for each; Biblical self-government has withered.

A society with Biblical self-government at its roots will be a society substantially free from oppressive rules and regulations. Only a people not self-governed under God will turn to a strong civil government to hold themselves in check. In truth, the people of a nation receive the type of government that their level of self-government deserves. What does this say about modern America?

CHAPTER 4

PROPERTY: STEWARDSHIP AND ACCOUNTABILITY

⌣

N oah Webster's 1828 dictionary defines property as "the exclusive right of possessing, enjoying, and disposing of a thing; ownership." Webster refused to stop with a prim and proper definition, however. As a committed Christian who hoped his dictionary might help educate Americans in Christian principles, he continued,

> In the beginning of the world, the Creator gave to man dominion over the earth, over the fish of the sea, and the fowls of the air, and over every living thing. This is the foundation of man's property in the earth and in all its productions.[1]

Property, therefore, in Webster's view, was not a human invention, but a right ordained by God. This corresponds exactly with Biblical teaching in the first chapter of Genesis:

And God blessed them [Adam and Eve]; and God said to them, "Be fruitful and multiply, and fill the earth, and subdue it; and rule over the fish of the sea and over the birds of the sky, and over every living thing that moves on the earth."[2]

Other Biblical passages state this dominion mandate as well. Psalm 8, for instance, includes a reaffirmation of Genesis 1:

Thou dost make him [man] to rule over the works of Thy hands; Thou hast put all things under his feet.[3]

God gave man the care of His property in an arrangement the Bible calls stewardship. A steward is a person employed to manage the concerns of another and is accountable to his employer. God made man a steward of His creation. Man is accountable to God for the manner in which he has possessed, enjoyed, and disposed of the property given to him. The principle of property is, quite simply, a principle of stewardship.

God takes the concept of stewardship seriously. The parable of the talents in Matthew 25 shows just how crucial stewardship is in God's purposes. A master about to go on a journey called his slaves and entrusted possessions to them. To one he gave five talents [a quantity of money], to another two, and to another, one. When he returned, he called them to account for their stewardship. The one to whom he gave five talents had doubled the amount; likewise the one who had been entrusted with two. The master was quite pleased and praised them.

Then he came to the slave who had been given one talent and the proceedings took a sharp turn. When confronted with his stewardship, the slave responded,

"Master, I knew you to be a hard man, reaping where you did not sow, and gathering where you scattered no seed. And I was afraid, and went away and hid your talent in the ground; see, you have what is yours." But his master answered and said to him, "You wicked, lazy slave, you knew that I reap where I did not sow, and gather where I scattered no seed? Then you ought to have put my money in the bank, and on my arrival I would have received my money back with interest. Therefore take away the talent from him, and give it to the one who has the ten talents." For to everyone who has shall more be given, and he shall have an abundance; but from the one who does not have, even what he does have shall be taken away. And cast out the worthless slave into the outer darkness; in that place there shall be weeping and gnashing of teeth.[4]

God apparently expects an increase on whatever He gives to man. It is not good enough simply to hang on to what one receives; one must use it profitably for the kingdom.

The Apostle Paul also enjoins stewardship:

Let a man regard us in this manner, as servants of Christ, and stewards of the mysteries of God. In this case, moreover, it is required of stewards that one be found trustworthy.[5]

All Christians are stewards of the gospel, commanded to share the message with all men. God will hold each Christian accountable for how he has handled the gospel message.

Properties—External and Internal

God has given men internal and external properties. As with the principles of individuality and self-government, the internal are more important, but it is worthwhile first to examine the external properties before discussing the internal.

The most obvious external property is oneself—the body that God has provided. Is it taken care of properly, or is it falling apart due to neglect or abuse? Proper nutrition and exercise are crucial to this stewardship. Although the body is temporary and Christians will receive a new body in the resurrection—one that won't deteriorate—God still is interested in its care. Lack of proper treatment of one's body may, at times, keep one from doing God's will.

The phrase "material possessions" covers many external properties. Money fits here, as well as all the things a person can buy with his money. What might God think of some possessions? Do they all honor Him or could some be considered dishonoring? Are they under control [self-governed] or have they become mini-gods that rule one's life? Money comes under the scrutiny of God's Word, the best-known caution being found in I Timothy:

> For the love of money is a root of all sorts of evil, and some by longing for it have wandered away from the faith, and pierced themselves with many a pang.[6]

People often turn the blessing of material possessions into a curse.

God also has given man the earth; stewardship of it is another requirement. The environmental movement has gone beyond stewardship to a mystical fascination with Mother Earth. Many environmentalists are part of the New Age Movement, which is Eastern mysticism in new packaging. Some of their beliefs derive from ancient pagan animism and fertility rites. The danger, though, is that Christians, repelled by environmental extremism, will neglect this stewardship. God wants His people to take the stewardship seriously, recognizing the earth as His gift, while rejecting the pagan approach to its preservation.

Time also is a valuable possession. God will hold each person accountable for its use. As the Apostle Peter writes:

> Therefore, since Christ has suffered in the flesh, arm yourselves also with the same purpose, because he who has suffered in the flesh has ceased from sin, so as to live the rest of the time in the flesh no longer for the lusts of men, but for the will of God.[7]

In other words, there is no time for sin; all time is subject to God's will. Part of God's will is leisure time, but He wants His people to lead productive lives. As Paul instructs Timothy concerning widows:

> But she who gives herself to wanton pleasure is dead even while she lives.... At the same time they also learn to be idle, as they go around from house to house; and not merely idle, but also gossips and busybodies, talking about things not proper to mention. Therefore, I want younger widows to get married, bear children, keep house, and give the enemy no occasion for reproach; for some have already turned aside to follow Satan.[8]

Idleness leads to sin. Paul's remedy is to concentrate on leading a productive life, using one's time wisely.

One's name and signature are properties. Both provide an identity and must be used with care. Anyone who carelessly attaches his signature to legal documents will learn accountability the hard way. This is why the book of Proverbs advises,

He who is surety for a stranger will surely suffer for it, but he who hates going surety is safe.... A man lacking in sense pledges, and becomes surety in the presence of his neighbor.[9]

A person becomes surety by co-signing another person's loan. If the borrower does not meet his obligations, the lender turns to the co-signer. The signature is legally binding. Just this one example should show that one's signature is a property to be handled cautiously.

Reputation is a property everyone possesses. Reputations can change. If one has made a commitment to Christ, concern for reputation should follow naturally. Of course, as with all properties, misuse is possible. Excessive concern for reputation can spring from vanity and purely selfish motives. Yet God does want His people to be aware that they represent Him. Among Paul's criteria for helping widows was that they have a "reputation for good works."[10] When the first deacons were chosen in the book of Acts, the apostles admonished that the church should

Select from among you, brethren, seven men of good **reputation**, full of the Spirit and of wisdom, whom we may put in charge of this task.[11]

There is, therefore, an appropriate concern for reputation, inspired by a regard for God's kingdom.

Each person possesses a heritage—through family and nation. Family heritage includes one's family history, and the culture, or "ways," handed down from previous generations. National heritage includes the form of government and the character and principles bequeathed by earlier generations. The liberty achieved by America's founding fathers is a property that must be used according to God's purposes. How is the current generation exercising this property? God holds each generation accountable, as well as each individual who is part of that generation.

Important as all these external properties are, the internal properties are more important. How one handles internal properties will determine how one handles external properties. God has graciously supplied man with at least the following internal properties: a spirit; a mind; emotions; talents or abilities; a free will; and a conscience. Each will be examined separately.

The spirit is that part of man that communes directly with the Lord. It is the part that goes on to be with Him after physical death. The book of Ecclesiastes declares that when people die,

> The dust [body] will return to the earth as it was, and the **spirit** will return to God who gave it.[12]

In the account of Jesus' death on the cross, the Bible reveals that "Jesus cried out again with a loud voice, and yielded up His spirit."[13] Therefore, the spirit is the essence of man that continues to exist even after what most people call "death." As Paul exclaims,

> The Spirit Himself bears witness with our **spirit** that we are children of God, and if children, heirs also, heirs of God and fellowheirs with Christ, if indeed we suffer with Him in order that we may also be glorified with Him.[14]

The spirit is a magnificent possession, but the stewardship of the other internal properties will determine its eternal destination.

The control of one's thought life was a key to victory in the previous discussion of self-government. Everything said in that discussion applies also to the property of the mind. The mind is a gift from God for which each person is accountable. Bad stewardship allows all kinds of evil thoughts to take root. Whatever goes into the mind eventually will alter one's character, either toward righteousness or toward sin. "For as he thinks within himself, so he is."[15] Good stewardship of the mind heeds Paul's counsel:

> Finally, brethren, whatever is true, whatever is honorable, whatever is right, whatever is pure, whatever is lovely, whatever is of good repute, if there is any excellence and if anything worthy of praise, let your **mind** dwell on these things.[16]

This is not humanistic positive thinking; it is wise stewardship.

I examined control of the emotions in the previous chapter. The only addition in the present discussion is the nature of those emotions as gifts from God. They are valuable properties. Misuse of these gifts can do eternal damage to the spirit. But if self-government is strong and emotions are handled properly, they can be an aid in keeping one focused on God and His purposes.

As the chapter on individuality revealed, God has given each person unique talents. All people are accountable to God for their use. Musical ability can serve either self or God. The same is true of administrative skills, teaching expertise, mechanical abilities—the list is long. It all comes down to the final two properties yet to be discussed: man's free will and his conscience.

The issue of free will has dominated theological debate almost from the beginning of the church age. I believe that Scripture teaches that man does possess a free will for which he is accountable. Some Christians make a distinction between a free will and a responsible will. I see no distinction. A man cannot be responsible if he is not free to choose. Accountability is meaningless without free will. Man can choose to follow God.

God told Moses and the children of Israel, "For this commandment which I command you today is not too difficult for you, nor is it out of reach."[17] He went on to say,

> I call heaven and earth to witness against you today, that I have set before you life and death, the blessing and the curse. So choose life in order that you may live, you and your descendants, by loving the Lord your God, by obeying His voice, and by holding fast to Him.[18]

Life and death, the blessing and the curse, have been set before everyone. Each individual must choose.

What an awesome responsibility, this free will! Couldn't God have made man in another way? No matter how one looks at it, man could have been created in only one of two ways—either with a free will or without one. But if God had excluded free will, He also would have excluded love. Without the capacity to choose, man becomes little more than a marionette, with all the strings pulled from above. The marionette does whatever the puppeteer decides. If the marionette acts lovingly, it is only because the puppeteer pulls the strings. It has no will of its own. Its "love" is meaningless.

When God created man with a free will, He took a tremendous risk because there was no guarantee that man would continue to use this gift according to His love. Yet God believed the risk was worthwhile when compared with the potential of loving relationships that would last throughout eternity. Love wants to share, and God, who is love, wanted to share His love with an entirely new type of being made in His image.

How was man to know what was loving and what was not? Another gift took care of that—the conscience.

Webster defines the conscience as "that faculty within us that makes decisions upon the lawfulness and unlawfulness of our actions, and instantly condemns or approves them." God placed the conscience within man for this purpose, so that man might know when he is following God's will and when He is not. I presume conscience was operating even before Adam and Eve sinned. As Eve pondered following the advice of Satan, there must have been a battle taking place within her because she knew the direct command of God that forbade her to do what Satan was suggesting. The tragedy is that she shook off what the conscience was telling her.

When man refuses to listen to his conscience, he sins. He misuses his free will and the eternal destination of his spirit is at risk. When one becomes well practiced at ignoring the conscience, dire consequences result, as Paul makes clear to Timothy:

> But the Spirit explicitly says that in later times some will fall away from the faith, paying attention to deceitful spirits and doctrines of demons, by means of the hypocrisy of liars seared in their own conscience as with a branding iron.[19]

People fall away from the faith because they sear their consciences. To sear is to make callous or hard. The image Paul impresses upon Timothy is that when a person stops listening to his conscience, a hardness develops in the moral sensibilities, and the conscience, for all practical purposes, becomes useless—it is no longer consulted. In some people, it may seem to have disappeared altogether. The conscience-seared person may commit horrendous sins without the least pang of guilt. The opposite is the Spirit-led individual whose conscience is finely tuned to the heart and mind of God; even the thought of committing sin leads to inward grief and turning away from the thought before it can find a home in his mind.

I have said that the internal is more important than the external and that the manner in which internal properties are handled will determine how external properties are handled. Only an individual who recognizes his spirit, mind, emotions, talents, free will, and conscience as gifts of God, and who exhibits self-government with these gifts, can be pleasing to God in the stewardship of external possessions.

Man's properties can be summarized as follows:

INTERNAL	EXTERNAL
Spirit Mind Emotions Talents Free Will CONSCIENCE	Body Material Possessions Earth Time Name and Signature Reputation Heritage

Property, Private Ownership, and Free Enterprise

An understanding of the role of private ownership of property and a comparison of economic systems is necessary before turning to the civil government's role in the principle of property. This is essential because one of the main components of government in the twentieth and twenty-first centuries has been its interaction [meddling?] with property (both internal and external) and the economy.

Based upon the principles of individuality, self-government, and the stewardship of property, one can make a strong case for a Biblical blessing on private owner-ship of property. In the parable of the talents mentioned earlier, there is no indication that possession of private property is wrong; in fact, the master desired an increase in his property. Although the parable's main purpose was to teach a spiritual principle, it is clear that God does not frown upon a person increasing his personal property.

"Thou shalt not steal" would be a strange compo-nent of the Ten Commandments if individuals were not allowed to have property. Stealing implies that one person has a right to a possession and another infringes upon that right. Moses told the Israelites,

> But you shall remember the Lord your God, for it is He who is giving you power to make wealth, that He may confirm His covenant which He swore to your fathers, as it is this day.[20]

Thus, God has ordained that man create wealth.

Neither money nor material possessions are sinful in themselves. Scripture speaks out against the rich only when they misuse their wealth. One looks in vain to see any kind of government scheme of redistribution. Some, though, claim that the Bible endorses communism, and rejects the right to private property. Does the Bible really teach that?

Support for Christian socialism or communism usu-ally is drawn from the book of Acts. For instance, one pas-sage says,

> And all those who had believed were together, and had all things in common; and they began selling their property and possessions, and were sharing them with all, as anyone might have need.[21]

To a generation raised on the teachings of Karl Marx, this sounds reminiscent of "from each according to his abilities, to each according to his needs." In the same book of Acts, two chapters later, are these words:

> And the congregation of those who believed were of one heart and soul; and not one of them claimed that anything belonging to him was his own; but all things were common property to them.... For there was not a needy person among them, for all who were owners of lands or houses would sell them and bring the proceeds of the sales, and lay them at the apostles' feet; and they would be distributed to each, as any had need.[22]

The next chapter then describes an incident that some feel confirms the communistic bent of the early church. Ananias and Sapphira sold some property, kept back some of the profit for themselves, and were struck dead for doing so. Surely, proponents of communism exclaim, this is evidence of God's displeasure with personal property. How should a Christian view this?

The first thing to notice is the tremendous distinction between the *voluntary* nature of the church enterprise and the *coerced* character of government redistribution of property. No one was forcing these early Christians to sell their property and give the proceeds to others; they were doing so out of a heart of love. Socialistic and communistic government operates quite differently. A law passes, an amount is forcibly withheld from paychecks, and each person thus makes his "contribution" to the needs of others. There is no personal relationship with the needy, no godly character required of the givers. They have no choice. In short, it is a violation of the principle of self-government.

Further, in the case of Ananias and Sapphira, they were not judged for holding back some of the money. A careful reading of the passage makes this undeniably clear.

> But a certain man named Ananias, with his wife Sapphira, sold a piece of property, and kept back some of the price for himself, with his wife's full knowledge, and bringing a portion of it, he laid it at the apostles' feet. But Peter said, "Ananias, why has Satan filled your heart to lie to the Holy Spirit, and to keep back some of the price of the land? While it remained unsold, did it not remain your own? And after it was sold, was it not under your control? Why is it that you have conceived this deed in your heart? You have not lied to men, but to God."[23]

Peter's indictment of Ananias was not that he had kept some money for himself, but that he had lied. He had tried to deceive the apostles into believing that the amount he was bringing was the entire profit from the sale, when in fact it was not. In other words, he was trying to make himself out to be something he wasn't; he was caught in pure hypocrisy. Peter even commented that the land was in Ananias's control before he sold it, meaning he had the right to decide how to use or dispose of it. After he sold it, the money was still his to use in whatever way he saw fit. The offense was that he lied.

A further confirmation of this interpretation is found a few verses later. When Sapphira arrived, unaware that her husband had died, Peter questioned her,

> "Tell me whether you sold the land for such and such a price?" And she said, "Yes, that was the price." Then Peter said to her, "Why is it that you have agreed together to put the Spirit of the Lord to the test? Behold,

the feet of those who have buried your husband are at the door, and they shall carry you out as well."[24]

Peter's question reveals that his concern was not that they had held back some money for themselves, but that they had lied about giving the whole amount, thereby creating a false impression. Ananias and Sapphira's deaths cannot be attributed to the private ownership of property, but to deception.

Only a system of private enterprise that allows private property is consistent with the principles of individuality and self-government. Without private ownership of property, men will not learn responsibility. Socialistic/communistic systems rob men of initiative, decision-making, and accountability for personal actions. The state becomes the provider instead of God.

Christians who promote socialism are substituting the government for God. They also are depriving God of one of His best teaching tools. The principle of property is God's school of accountability. If men do not have property for which they are accountable, they never learn individual self-government. They never mature and cannot be trusted with further responsibilities.

Human experience has shown numerous examples of the folly of the communist experiment. When the Pilgrims arrived in the New World, their agreement with the financial backers of their venture included a provision that they farm the land in common. The results were disastrous. As William Bradford, the governor of the Plymouth colony and author of Plymouth's history explains,

> The failure of this experiment of communal living, which was tried for several years, and by good and honest men proves the emptiness of the theory of Plato and other ancients, applauded by some of later times—that the taking away of private property, and

the possession of it in community, by a common-wealth, would make a state happy and flourishing; as if they were wiser than God. For in this instance, community of property ... was found to breed much confusion and discontent, and retard much employment which would have been to the general benefit and comfort. For the young men who were most able and fit for service objected to being forced to spend their time and strength in working for other men's wives and children, without any recompense. The strong man or the resourceful man had no more share of food, clothes, etc., than the weak man who was not able to do a quarter the other could. This was thought injustice. The aged and graver men, who were ranked and equalized in labor, food, clothes, etc., with the humbler and younger ones, thought it some indignity and disrespect to them. As for men's wives who were obliged to do service for other men, such as cooking, washing their clothes, etc., they considered it a kind of slavery, and many husbands would not brook it. This feature of it would have been worse still, if they had been men of an inferior class [i.e., not good Christians].

... Let none argue that this is due to human failing, rather than to this communistic plan of life in itself. I answer, seeing that all men have this failing in them, that God in His wisdom saw that another course was fitter for them.[25]

Bradford introduced private property for families. Initiative returned, productivity increased, and the settlers became responsible farmers again.

The twentieth century experienced an almost giddy love affair with the socialist/communist system. But by the beginning of the century's last decade, the fruit of that system became evident to most. The leading proponent of the system, the Soviet Union, was on the brink of economic collapse. Its satellite states in eastern Europe, suffering from the same type of collapse, were able to take advantage of Soviet weakness to break away and form new governments, some of them committed (at least in word) to free enterprise. The socialist vision, however, dies hard. It remains to be seen whether these countries truly will escape its phony allures.

Property and Civil Government

Civil government must respect private property in order for people to prosper materially. But respect for private property must go beyond the economic realm. As the showdown in China's Tiananmen Square in 1989 revealed, economic liberty also must incorporate other liberties. The Chinese government tried to open itself to economic freedom while continuing to repress other freedoms, only to discover that liberty—self-government—cannot be divided. Liberty of conscience in both the religious and political areas is indissolubly linked with economic liberty.

When the American colonies became alarmed by the economic policies of the British government, they were not concerned only with their pocketbooks. They declared time and again that he who had the power to tax also had the power to control every aspect of people's lives. This was why they pushed for self-government based upon representation. Stephen Hopkins, Rhode Island governor and signer of the Declaration of Independence, stated as early as 1764,

> Those who are governed at the will of another, or of others, and whose property may be taken from them by taxes or otherwise without their own consent and against their will, are in the miserable condition of slaves.[26]

Hopkins's view was that the property of consent [free will] was in danger if men lost control of their external possessions. Absolute control of what one owns leads to absolute control of the owners.

James Madison, the Father of the Constitution and fourth president of the United States, wrote an article on property in 1792 that probably best summarizes how extensive a person's property is, and the government's responsibility toward that property. Madison's explanation of property comes very close to the internal and external properties discussed earlier in this chapter. Property, he says,

> embraces every thing to which a man may attach a value and have a right; and *which leaves to every one else the like advantage.* [emphasis Madison's]
>
> In the former sense, a man's land, or merchandize, or money is called his property.
>
> In the latter sense, a man has a property in his opinions and the free communication of them.
>
> He has a property of peculiar value in his religious opinions, and in the profession and practice dictated by them.
>
> He has a property very dear to him in the safety and liberty of his person.
>
> He has an equal property in the free use of his faculties and free choice of the objects on which to employ them.
>
> In a word, as a man is said to have right to his property, he may be equally said to have a property in his rights.[27]

He then continues with government's responsibility toward each man's rights:

> Where an excess of power prevails, property of no sort is duly respected. No man is safe in his opinions, his person, his faculties, or his possessions....
>
> Government is instituted to protect property of every sort; ... This being the end of government, that alone is a *just* government, which *impartially* secures to every man, whatever is his *own*.

Notice how he links opinions, person, faculties, and possessions as if they are one. Just government secures these. How can one identify unjust government?

> That is not a just government, nor is property secure under it, where the property which a man has in his personal safety and personal liberty, is violated by arbitrary seizures of one class of citizens for the service of the rest.

His description of unjust government continues:

> That is not a just government, nor is property secure under it, where arbitrary restrictions, exemptions, and monopolies deny to part of its citizens that free use of their faculties, and free choice of their occupations....
>
> A just security to property is not afforded by that government, under which unequal taxes oppress one species of property and reward another species: where arbitrary taxes invade the domestic sanctuaries of the rich, and excessive taxes grind the faces of the poor.

Government then, according to Madison, must secure men's properties and must provide a political climate in which men are free from arbitrary seizures of their persons and possessions [external] and their faculties and free choice [internal]. He concludes his article with a warning to the fledgling government of America:

> If there be a government then which prides itself in maintaining the inviolability of property; which provides that none shall be taken *directly* even for public use without indemnification to the owner, and yet *directly* violates the property which individuals have in their opinions, their religion, their persons, and their faculties ... such a government is not a pattern for the United States.

> If the United States mean to obtain or deserve the full praise due to wise and just governments, they will equally respect the rights of property, and the property in rights: they will rival the government that most sacredly guards the former; and be repelling its example in violating the latter, will make themselves a pattern to that and all other governments.

Madison's views are no different from what has been expressed elsewhere in this chapter. But he applies them to civil government. Only a government that safeguards the "inviolability of property" can be said to be operating on a Biblical principle.

Conscience and Civil Government

Of all man's internal properties, conscience, as stated previously, is the most important. The conscience lets man know right and wrong. Refusal to listen leads to misuse of free will and eternal consequences. Madison, in the same article on property, recognizes this truth when he admonishes,

Conscience is the most sacred of all property; other property depending in part on positive law, the exercise of that, being a natural and unalienable right. To guard a man's house as his castle, to pay public and enforce private debts with the most exact faith, can give no title to invade a man's conscience which is more sacred than his castle, or to withhold from it that debt of protection, for which the public faith is pledged, by the very nature and original conditions of the social pact.

Government, according to Madison, must protect a man's liberty of conscience. Even his home is not as important as his conscience. This is in accord with the Biblical understanding of conscience.

Governments have violated liberty of conscience throughout history; denial of liberty of conscience has been the norm. When the apostles started preaching the gospel, they were put in prison. When told to cease teaching about Jesus, they responded, "We must obey God rather than men."[28] If they had obeyed the human authority, they would have disobeyed God. By staying faithful to the higher authority, they maintained liberty of conscience in God's sight even though they suffered at the hands of men.

One of the most detrimental developments in church history was the union of church and state that took place under Constantine and extended even into the modern era. Civil government and church government formed a coalition to stifle any belief that tended to undermine the established hierarchy in both religious and political realms. When Martin Luther stood against the prevailing wisdom in the sixteenth century, he was not just attacking church doctrine; he also was laying the axe to the existing political arrangement. Yet he stood firm and maintained liberty of conscience toward God.

Once the Protestant Reformation took root in England, the political and religious authorities again attempted to determine orthodoxy and threatened to punish dissenters. Puritans and Separatists dissented anyway. Many suffered for their positions; others fled to the New World where they could have the liberty of conscience they desired.

The specter of totalitarian government has dominated both the twentieth and twenty-first centuries. In socialist states religion has been either downplayed or forbidden. Their governments have suppressed political opinions that differ from those of the parties in power.

The United States is not a fully socialized state, yet evidence is mounting that there is pressure from government to believe certain ideas and to disregard others. College campuses are passing regulations dictating what can and cannot be said about certain groups of people (homosexuals, women, minorities of all types). Conservatives have condemned this push for politically correct speech, but socialist elements have the upper hand in academia; only those on the left of the political spectrum seem to enjoy liberty of conscience on many campuses.

The educational system as a whole has relegated Biblical beliefs to a mere historical footnote (and not a very savory one at that) and the "religion" of humanism has been the only one allowed to benefit from government funding. Yet the constant drumbeat of rhetoric suggests that America is a "pluralistic" nation in which everyone has liberty of conscience. This assertion bears some scrutiny, but first it is necessary to see how liberty of conscience exists throughout society, for Christian and non-Christian alike.

Biblical liberty of conscience begins with the individual's relationship to God. A person cannot be a Christian without certain basic beliefs. Yet there are other areas where God allows liberty of conscience. The best chapter on this is Romans 14, in which Paul deals with individual conscience on matters such as food, drink, and outward observances. His conclusion?

> The faith which you have, have as your own conviction before God. Happy is he who does not condemn himself in what he approves. But he who doubts is condemned if he eats, because his eating is not from faith; and whatever is not from faith is sin.[29]

Each Christian, therefore, must find peace with God concerning those nonessential matters.

He then finds others who share his beliefs, as nearly as possible. He may not find the "perfect" church. The best one available may not be in total agreement with his views, but he can feel comfortable with its direction and purpose. Already, he is learning that he must offer liberty of conscience to fellow believers. Other churches will be farther from his ideal, yet he and the people in his local congregation can sometimes join with them in areas of broad agreement. The willingness to work with those who are farther afield from some personal convictions broadens the scope of liberty of conscience.

Thus far, the discussion has focused on the church. A country such as the United States is made up of diverse peoples, most of whom are not Christians. Neither can they be forced to accept the Christian way because that would violate liberty of conscience. All historical attempts to "create" Christians by force have only bred hypocrisy. Christians and non-Christians live under the same government. They all have the same rights, and liberty of conscience must be respected.

Yet consciences can be educated and influenced. Christians, whose liberty of conscience is just as sacred as that of non-Christians, should be free to influence others toward the Christian worldview. All societies have a standard. Christians can raise their standard and use all legitimate educational and political means to promote that standard for their country. Non-Christians are free to do the same.

Pluralism is a different concept altogether. The basis for modern pluralism is *moral relativism*. Those who advocate pluralism usually don't believe in absolute truth. They say that all views receive equal treatment, but there is a concerted effort to censor any view that promotes absolutes. In the guise of pluralism, Christian influence is denounced as "trying to legislate morality." The assumption is that morality cannot be legislated. Is that true?

What is a law? Every law is a statement by the political community declaring certain actions to be wrong and others to be right. Lawbreakers receive penalties. Obviously, these laws are not simply suggestions. Whenever one is dealing with right and wrong, morality is the issue. All laws are moral. Even the stop sign on the corner is a moral statement: "Refuse to stop here and you will be penalized. It is wrong to drive past here without stopping because the community has deemed it unsafe to the lives and property of other individuals." Therefore, it is *wrong* not to stop.

The idea that morality cannot be legislated masks an agenda: the replacement of Christian principles of government and society with humanistic principles. The Christian response cannot be to force the Christian viewpoint, but it can be a wholehearted attempt to reeducate society in Biblical principles.

Property used to be a cornerstone of American government. The onslaught of socialist thought in the twentieth century has weakened this cornerstone considerably. The apostles said they had to obey God rather than men. Martin Luther stood for truth even when he thought it would cost his life. The Separatists became Pilgrims and set up a government and society based upon Biblical principles. It is time for another generation of Christians to maintain liberty of conscience before God and stop the erosion of the Christian principle of property—both internal and external. We have a stewardship. We are accountable to God.

CHAPTER 5

UNITY AND UNION: VOLUNTARINESS AND DIVERSITY

Individuality, self-government, property—all these principles have emphasized the individual, although some applications have been made to society. But the individual does not exist in a vacuum. The same God who made the individual the cornerstone of society also made society—individuals who must function together to achieve common purposes. God arranged His creation to reflect both the individual and the society. The individual does not exist apart from society, but neither does society swallow up the individual. Both are necessary for God's purposes.

Unity and union is a complement to individuality. It reveals how unique individuals with their distinct identities can work together. The goal is *unity with diversity*, not uniformity. As with individuality, the example of the body of Christ in I Corinthians 12 explains it best when it states that the body is not one member, but many, and that each member has a specific function.

There are several ideas in this passage relevant to the principle of unity and union. Diversity, however, is the main focus. The body of Christ is composed of many different types of people—Jews, Greeks, slaves, and free— with differing gifts. Paul uses the analogy of the natural body throughout his description, but one can substitute other terminology. For example, one might complain, "Because I am not a pastor, I am not really a part of the body." The message is that no matter what function a person performs, he is a significant part of Christ's body. God doesn't need three hundred pastors in each congregation. He also needs people who have a heart for taking care of others' material needs, for exercising an unseen, unheralded prayer ministry, or for cleaning the church building.

> And God has appointed in the church, first apostles, second prophets, third teachers, then miracles, then gifts of healings, helps, administrations, various kinds of tongues. All are not apostles, are they? All are not prophets, are they? All are not teachers, are they? All are not workers of miracles, are they? All do not have gifts of healings, do they? All do not speak with tongues, do they? All do not interpret, do they?[1]

There is a unique purpose for each person in the body, thus maintaining the principle of individuality; yet there is a unity in the midst of the diversity.

Unity and union. Aren't they the same? Both the dictionary and Scripture make a distinction. Unity is voluntary agreement that takes place in the heart among individuals. Union is the act of joining two or more things into one. Therefore, unity is the *internal* aspect of this principle, while union is the *external*. A union is the external arrangement that results from internal unity.

Unity and union means: external unions must be built upon internal unity and be voluntary to succeed; union thrives on diversity as each individual offers his uniqueness to the union; unity must precede union for the union to be effective; union without unity will ultimately fail because of its superficiality. I believe Scripture supports this statement of the principle, as just a few examples will show.

The prophet Amos asserts, "Do two men walk together unless they have made an agreement?"[2] In context, Amos uses this as the first of a series of seven declarations for which he does not expect an argument. In other words, he uses it as a rhetorical device, assuming its truth. His point is simply this: no union can be formed unless it is preceded by internal unity.

Paul affirms Amos when he tells the church at Corinth,

> Do not be bound together with unbelievers; for what partnership have righteousness and lawlessness, or what fellowship has light with darkness? Or what harmony has Christ with Belial, or what has a believer in common with an unbeliever? Or what agreement has the temple of God with idols? For we are the temple of the living God.[3]

He uses the words "partnership," "fellowship," "harmony," and "agreement," all words indicating an internal condition. The message is, if internal unity is not present, do not form an external union.

Salvation is another example of unity and union. It cannot occur until a man first agrees with God concerning his own sinfulness, his need for repentance, and for faith in Jesus. Once he reaches internal agreement, repents of his sins and declares his faith in the work of Jesus, he is able to form a union, or relationship, with God because of the internal unity that preceded it. Any attempt to shortcut internal unity will result in a false salvation experience. Internal agreement is essential before the external union can exist.

Unity and Union—External Unions and Internal Agreements Identified

There are so many possibilities of external unions that only a sampling will be possible. Friendship is a bond between individuals. It has no legal status, but it is a union. Proverbs notes the bonding aspect of friendship in the comment, "A friend loves at all times."[4] Marriage, on the other hand, goes beyond friendship and is a legal external partnership. The marriage union was recognized in the book of Genesis and repeated by Jesus:

> For this cause a man shall leave his father and his mother and shall cleave to his wife; and they shall become one flesh.[5]

Jesus stressed the importance of this union when He admonished, "What therefore God has joined together, let no man separate."[6]

Clubs or organizations in which individuals unite for a specific purpose, whether a school science club, Future Teachers of America, the Kiwanis Club, Jaycees, or a labor union, are unions. Governments are unions. Sometimes they are not voluntary, but they are unions because they control and direct a group of people living in a certain geographic region.

Unity is vital for any of these unions to be effective. What kind of unity is necessary to make a union strong and productive?

Beliefs [or convictions], purposes [or goals], and interests are logical candidates for internal agreement. A person must believe what God reveals to him and change his purpose from serving self to serving God to experience salvation. From then on, his interests will coincide with God's interests. Paul highlights internal agreement in his letters. To the Corinthians he writes,

> Now I exhort you, brethren, by the name of our Lord Jesus Christ, that you all agree, and there be no divisions among you, but you be made complete in the same mind and in the same judgment.[7]

To the Philippians he remarks:

> If therefore there is any encouragement in Christ, if there is any consolation of love, if there is any fellowship of the Spirit, if any affection and compassion, make my joy complete by being of the same mind, maintaining the same love, united in spirit, intent on one purpose.[8]

Both are clarion calls for *agreement*. In both, Paul talks about having the *same mind*. In the Philippians passage, he mentions unity of *purpose*. Obviously, he is concerned that a church that lacks this internal unity will not hold together externally.

The Philippians passage also talks about unity of spirit, that is, the necessity of each individual human spirit being in unity through the Holy Spirit. Paul explains in Ephesians:

> I, therefore, the prisoner of the Lord, entreat you to walk in a manner worthy of the calling with which you have been called, with all humility and gentleness, with patience, showing forbearance to one another in

love, being diligent to preserve the unity of the Spirit in the bond of peace.[9]

He then extols the diversity in the body of Christ and how the diversity is meant to lead to an even greater unity:

> And He gave some as apostles, and some as prophets, and some as evangelists, and some as pastors and teachers, for the equipping of the saints for the work of service to the building up of the body of Christ; until we all attain to the unity of the faith, and of the knowledge of the Son of God, to a mature man, to the measure of the stature which belongs to the fullness of Christ.[10]

"Unity of the faith" is agreement in beliefs. This occurs through the diversity of ministries in the church. Diversity is not a threat, but a help.

I have discussed the ideal. What about unions that do not have sufficient internal unity, or unions in which the unity is forced?

Some perceived friendships are not true friendships. Proverbs warns: "A man of many friends comes to ruin, but there is a friend who sticks closer than a brother."[11] True and false friendships are both mentioned in this verse. It is important to know why someone claims to be a friend. Is the attraction internal—unity of belief, purpose, interests—or is it self-serving in some way? Selfishness at the root of a "friendship" is the seed of its destruction.

A key to a successful marriage is sharing beliefs, purposes, and interests. American society is witnessing a deterioration of strong marriages. The main reason for this, besides acceptance of easy divorce, is the lack of unity. Marriages are built on wrong foundations. Often physical attraction dominates a man's reason for wanting to marry. A woman latches onto security in the marriage contract. Both rationales are external. In twenty years, when his wife is no longer as young and appealing, the husband may look elsewhere. When the wife begins to feel that her husband doesn't understand her, she may seek a tender spirit in another man.

Marriage counseling should begin before marriage with the principle of unity and union. Does the couple share the same convictions? If so, are both looking at the same goals in life? Just because two people are Christians doesn't mean their marriage is "made in heaven." One may wish to serve God in a way that would be contrary to the direction the other believes God is leading. They would be at cross purposes. Even if the purposes were identical, they might have so many different interests [hobbies, etc.] that a large hole might appear in the marriage in later years. All internal factors need to be considered before making a marriage decision.

Church splits are common. Doctrinal differences crop up. Half the church feels led to minister in one direction, while the other half senses the opposite. As explained in the last chapter, each individual has liberty of conscience and should join himself to the church that is closest to his own beliefs, purposes, and interests.

The union of church and state in the Roman Empire was a disaster not only for self-government and liberty of conscience, but also for unity and union. An ecclesiastical organization grew that defined the institution of the church very narrowly. Salvation came only through membership. It created a union held together only by force because many people's hearts were not united with the church's beliefs and purposes. Eventually this structure cracked, and the Reformation shattered the illusion of a genuine union.

Rome itself is another example of a failed union. It lasted a long time, but only because it had the military might to control its conquered provinces. The people of those conquered provinces did not possess internal unity with Rome. If there was an opportunity to escape its clutches, some would take it. The Jewish revolt from 66-70 A.D. is one example. There were too many different beliefs and nationalities under the Roman umbrella for it to last forever.

A modern empire that mirrors the Roman experience is the late Soviet Union. Created by force, the Soviet Union finally had to face its lack of internal unity. The Russian people dominated this "union," and other peoples did not want to be part of it. The revolt began with its satellite countries. The failure of the socialist program and the desire to express nationalistic individuality led to a breakup of the Warsaw Pact. These events happened so quickly in the fall of 1989 and early 1990 that they took nearly everyone by surprise.

Then the revolt hit home. Conquered provinces within the Soviet Union clamored for independence. Lithuania, Latvia, and Estonia decried their forced entry into the system in the 1940s. Finally, even the section known as Armenia, which voluntarily entered the union in the 1920s, decided to leave. In 1992, the Soviet Union transformed itself into the Commonwealth of Independent States. It will last only if it maintains sufficient internal unity.

The internal and external aspects of unity and union can be listed as follows:

INTERNAL	EXTERNAL
Beliefs/Convictions Purposes/Goals Interests Spirit	Friendship Marriage Church Club Labor Union Government

Unity and Union in the Formation of the United States

Early American history offers an excellent illustration of unity and union. Rarely does a historical example so clearly show the development of a unity that led to a viable political union.

The Pilgrims and Puritans were people with strong unity of belief and purpose. The Puritans, when they began arriving in great numbers in the 1630s, literally believed they were on a divine mission to set up a city on a hill, to become a light to old England, revealing God's way for ordering church and society.

The first union they established that went beyond separate settlements was the New England Confederacy that lasted from 1643 to 1684. The basis for this confederacy was theological agreement, and it respected the right of each settlement to remain a self-governing entity.

When James II took the throne in 1685, he attempted to create an artificial union in the New World. James did not appreciate the Puritanism of the New England colonies and sought to force them back into Anglicanism. He created the Dominion of New England, a centralized government incorporating Massachusetts, Connecticut, Plymouth, Rhode Island, and New York.

This centralization was a denial of the right of self-government, but it also was a violation of unity and union because most of the colonists had no unity of belief or purpose with the Anglican Church. The colonies resisted this oppression and ultimately threw off the Dominion after the English dethroned James in the "Glorious Revolution" of 1688. Self-government was restored.

After the failure of the Dominion of New England, each American colony gloried in its individuality and self-government. There was no external union. A citizen of Virginia, for example, did not call himself an American, but a Virginian. Virginia was his country. American national consciousness was nonexistent.

The first written proposal for union came from William Penn, founder of Pennsylvania. His 1698 plan was entitled, "A brief and plain scheme whereby the English colonies may be made more useful to the crown and one another's peace and safety with an universal concurrence." He proposed that the colonies send representatives to an annual meeting "to debate and resolve of such measures as are most advisable for their better understanding and the public tranquillity and safety."[12] Penn appears to have been the only person interested.

The initial step in the formation of unity in the colonies came from God. It was called the Great Awakening. The Awakening was a revival of the Christian faith that began sporadically in the 1720s and extended into the 1740s. It began in local self-governing communities, as the Spirit of God reawakened people to their individual accountability for salvation.

The climax came in 1740 with the arrival of evangelist George Whitefield, who came ashore in Georgia and traversed the entire eastern seaboard, preaching the Word of God with powerful effect. Through Whitefield, the Awakening became a multi-colony experience. Whole cities came to a standstill to hear him. Even Benjamin Franklin, who never became a Christian convert, was impressed with the results of Whitefield's time in Philadelphia. Franklin commented, "It was wonderful to see the change soon made in the manners of our inhabitants; from being thoughtless or indifferent about religion, it seemed as if all the world were growing religious, so that one could not walk thro' the town in an evening without hearing psalms sung in different families of every street."[13]

Historians have disagreed over the actual results of this Awakening. Some point to denominational splits and conclude that it did not create unity. Yet I believe the general effect was positive. Many new colleges started, colleges dedicated to Christian scholarship and to applying the Christian faith to all walks of life. Princeton, Brown, Rutgers, and Dartmouth all trace their beginnings to the Awakening.

Although some critiqued the Awakening's external methods (British colonials were not used to emotional religion), many were shaken from their lethargy concerning the need for individual salvation. The message of personal response to God was preached in every colony, and the Awakening became the first truly "American" event, shared by every colony. It created a sense of American unity of spirit that prepared the way for eventual political unity and union.

In 1754, British officials, concerned about France's claims in the New World, pushed for colonial union. They announced a convention to be held in Albany, New York, to discuss a union "for their mutual defence and security, and for extending the British Settlements in North America."[14] Franklin, at that time publisher of the *Philadelphia Gazette* newspaper, promoted the Albany Plan of Union with the motto, "Join or Die," but only seven colonies sent representatives. The only enthusiasm for the plan came from royal officials; American colonists saw no need for a union. Without internal unity, there is no sense trying to create a union.

The Albany Plan, however, did create discussion of union in colonial assemblies, particularly with the onset of the French and Indian War in 1756. Union, some argued, would help in self-defense. Yet the strong attachment to self-government defeated any plan for union. The desire for self-government, in this case, was bordering on self-ishness—a lack of concern for the good of all people in the American colonies.

The colonies might have continued in this vein if it had not been for a change of policy in the British government. In 1765, when the Parliament first attempted to tax the colonies directly, the colonial people shook off their complacency. The Stamp Act raised a furor. The threat to self-government and property, and the birth of unity of purpose, led to a union to deal with the situation.

Massachusetts took the lead in calling for a congress of representatives from all the colonies

> ... to consult together on the present circumstances of the colonies, and the difficulties to which they are and must be reduced by the operation of the late acts of Parliament for levying duties and taxes on the colonies, and to consider of a general and humble address to his Majesty and the Parliament, to implore relief.[15]

The Stamp Act Congress met on 7 October 1765 and signed a petition calling for repeal of the act. There also was much resistance to the Stamp Act in Great Britain because the British merchants feared that their profits might suffer if the American colonies retaliated with a boycott. So Parliament repealed the act before its scheduled effective date. For the first time, the colonists became

Americans. The Stamp Act Congress signaled the initial political step of union among the colonies.

The repeal, however, was not a victory for the principles in which the colonists believed. Parliament did not accept the argument that taxation without representation was a violation of self-government and property. Attached to the repeal was a new act, the Declaratory Act (1766), which proclaimed that Parliament had the right to pass any laws for the colonies that it saw fit to enact, and that the colonies were bound to obey. This British attitude led to another confrontation.

In 1767 the British attempted again to place direct taxes on the colonies. The Townshend Acts were laws levying taxes on tea, lead, paper, and glass. To ensure compliance, the government sent troops to Boston, the seat of the resistance. Upon passage of these acts, all the colonies again rose in protest.

One Pennsylvania resistance leader, John Dickinson, identified the problem succinctly in his "Farmer's Letter to the Inhabitants of the British Colonies." Dickinson wrote:

> Some persons may think this act of no consequence, because the duties are so small. A fatal error. That is the very circumstance most alarming to me. For I am convinced, that the authors of this law would never have obtained an act to raise so trifling a sum as it must do, had they not intended by it to establish a precedent for future use. To console ourselves with the smallness of the duties, is to walk deliberately into the snare that is set for us.... In short, if they have a right to levy a tax of one penny upon us, they have a right to levy a million upon us: for where does their right stop?[16]

Self-government and property were at the heart of his concern. He then appealed for unity and union:

Let us consider ourselves as men—freemen—Christian freemen—separated from the rest of the world, and firmly bound together by the same rights, interests and dangers. Let these keep our attention inflexibly fixed on the great objects, which we must continually regard, in order to preserve those rights, to promote those interests, and to avert those dangers.[17]

The colonists were Christian freemen, asserted Dickinson, bound together by a unity of belief in their rights and by a unity of interests. A solution to the problem lay in attacking it together. He believed God supported this thinking:

On such emergencies you may surely, without presumption believe, that Almighty God himself will look down upon your righteous contest with gracious approbation. You will be a "band of brothers," cemented by the dearest ties, and strengthened with inconceivable supplies of force and constancy, by that sympathetic ardor, which animates good men, confederated in a good cause.[18]

A "band of brothers," Dickinson called his countrymen, "cemented" together and "confederated" in a good cause. Both internal unity and external union were parts of his plea.

The Massachusetts assembly, in 1768, sent a petition to King George III and a Circular Letter to the other colonies. The Letter's purpose was to create unity among the colonies. It took issue with the taxes and promoted a colonial boycott of British goods. The king and the Massachusetts governor put severe pressure on the assembly to rescind the letter, but when the vote came, the unity and union of the Massachusetts legislators was too strong to break, and they refused to comply. This, of course, made Massachusetts the prime target of British actions from that time forward.

The colonies drew up a boycott agreement. Although there was not total unanimity in carrying out the agreement, the degree of compliance hurt the British merchants. These merchants petitioned Parliament for repeal of the Townshend taxes. Parliament, in 1770, under pressure from the merchants, repealed every tax except the one on tea. Again, colonial unity and union had secured a victory of sorts, but the tax on tea was retained as a symbol that Parliament still did not agree with the colonial position. It was in the same spirit as the Declaratory Act.

Repeal of the taxes brought a sense of relief to the colonists, many of whom wanted trade as usual. The tea tax was a nuisance, but most were willing to ignore it. A false security about future relations with the British government lulled them to sleep. The period from 1770 to 1773 was one of relative external peace. Yet those who understood the principles on which the colonists had taken their stand knew that nothing had been resolved.

Samuel Adams was one such man. Adams inaugurated the Committees of Correspondence, designed to promote unity and union among the colonies. These committees were set up first in the towns of Massachusetts. They then spread to other colonies with two goals: to keep each colony informed on the latest British actions, and to educate in the principles that formed the foundation of their resistance. Legislatures in twelve of the colonies appointed committees of correspondence. These committees kept the principles before the minds of the people and helped forge the unity that was very quickly heading toward union.

A single incident brought the whole matter to a head. In 1773 Parliament passed the Tea Act. This act tried to help the ailing East India Tea Company by allowing it to import tea directly to America without going through Britain, omitting some of the cost to the company. This looked good for the colonists because the tea would be cheaper, but those who knew the principles at stake opposed the landing of any tea. They knew that the tax was still on it, and they also saw that this policy undercut colonial merchants, giving the East India Tea Company a virtual monopoly. In other words, they opposed a lower price because it would have violated self-government and property.

This opposition led to the Boston Tea Party on 16 December 1773. The destruction of the tea has caused many to consider the Tea Party inexcusable. But the captain of the ships stood to lose those ships unless he landed the tea. If he had tried to leave Boston with the tea still aboard, his ships would have been impounded. Resistance leaders decided to divest the captain of his cargo, allowing him to leave without penalty. No other property was destroyed and, by all accounts, the whole matter progressed quickly and solemnly, evidencing a controlled protest rather than a riot.

The British overreacted to the Tea Party by passing laws that punished Massachusetts severely. They closed the Boston port to commerce in an attempt to starve the "rebellious" inhabitants. No longer could the people elect the second branch of the legislature or choose judges. The governor now controlled appointments for both. Town meetings, the lifeblood of New England self-government, were restricted to once a year for the sole purpose of electing public officials; discussion of issues by the people was forbidden. Anyone accused of opposing the governor would be sent to Britain for trial. Private homes could now be used to quarter British troops, without the consent of the owners. These acts amounted to a full-fledged tyranny—a cancellation of all semblance of self-government.

The British response couldn't have been more ill-advised. The harshness of this response, intended to teach Massachusetts a lesson and warn all the other colonies against similar actions, had the opposite effect. Once the rest of the colonies realized the impact of the laws against Massachusetts, they understood that *their* self-government and property were at risk. British measures cemented the last bricks into the wall of colonial union.

Colonial legislatures met and passed resolutions. They sent food and supplies to Boston to thwart the Port Bill. Virginia called for a day of fasting, humiliation, and prayer. The words of that resolution acknowledge the importance of internal unity in the American union. It called on citizens

> ... devoutly to implore the divine interposition, for averting the heavy calamities which threatened destruction to their civil rights, and the evils of a civil war; and to give them **one heart and mind**, to oppose, by all just and proper means, every injury to American rights.[19]

Finally, the colonies called for a Continental Congress to meet and discuss a unified colonial response.

The assembling of the Continental Congress in Philadelphia in September 1774 was the final link of unity and union. Without this step, armed resistance would have been impossible. When the Congress met, it spoke with a clear and virtually undivided voice. It declared the British acts against Massachusetts to be unconstitutional; resistance was necessary. It again explained the rights of the colonists regarding self-government and property, and set up an embargo of all British goods. This Continental Congress met continually after hostilities began and served as a national government during the American Revolution.

The most significant document to emanate from the Continental Congress was the Declaration of Independence, the main part of which was a catalog of the abuses of the British crown. But the introduction and the conclusion reveal it to be a document based upon the principles of individuality, self-government, property, and unity and union.[20]

The second paragraph identifies God as the creator of all men. It declares that He endowed man with "certain unalienable Rights, that among these, are Life, Liberty, and the pursuit of Happiness." The right to life corresponds to individuality because that principle emphasizes that God created each person unique and distinct with a particular purpose. The right to life is essential for that purpose to be fulfilled. The right to liberty includes self-government and property, since private property and liberty of conscience are indispensable ingredients of the latter.

The pursuit of happiness is not the twenty-first-century version, but that of British jurist William Blackstone, the writer all American lawyers studied for their understanding of law. Blackstone identified happiness as doing God's will when he explained, "For He [God] has so intimately connected, so inseparably interwoven the laws of eternal justice with the happiness of each individual, that the latter cannot be attained but by observing the former; and, if the former be punctually obeyed, it cannot but induce the latter."[21] The founders' concept of happiness, therefore, was tied to obedience to God's law, a concept almost totally missing in modern America.

The Declaration is a testimony to unity and union, the final act cementing the individual states into a confederated body. The last paragraph proclaims,

We, therefore, the Representatives of the united States of America, in General Congress assembled, appealing to the Supreme Judge of the World for the rectitude of our intentions, do, in the Name, and by Authority of the good People of these Colonies, solemnly Publish and Declare, That these United Colonies are, and of Right, ought to be free and Independent States; that they are Absolved from all Allegiance to the British Crown, and that all political connexion between them and the State of Great Britain, is and ought to be totally dissolved; and that, as Free and Independent States, they have full Power to levy War, conclude Peace, contract Alliances, establish Commerce, and to do all other Acts and Things which Independent States may of right do. And for the support of this Declaration, with a firm reliance on the protection of divine Providence, we mutually pledge to each other our Lives, our Fortunes, and our sacred Honour.

Note the wording: the "united States of America"; "in General Congress assembled"; "these United Colonies." Also note the absolving of all allegiance to the British crown, signifying the end of one union and the initiation of another. Finally, each signatory to the document agreed to "mutually pledge to each other our Lives, our Fortunes, and our sacred Honour." That is an indication of how united they had become. They joined together in a common cause or purpose; it manifested itself in a new political union.

The war, and the peace that followed, proved to be rigorous tests for American unity and union. The trials of conflict may just as often tear men apart as draw them together. Once the danger is removed, many retreat from alliances they formed when the danger was clear and present.

America suffered a crisis of unity and union in the years immediately following the conclusion of the war. The government set up by the Articles of Confederation was too weak and lacked the respect of the people it was supposed to govern. Unity of belief concerning the need to strengthen this government brought political leaders together from every colony except Rhode Island to form a union that we now call the Constitutional Convention.

Delegates to the Constitutional Convention, which met in Philadelphia from May to September in 1787, brought diverse ideas with them concerning the future of the American republic. Near the end of June it appeared that the Convention might dissolve in failure. At this critical juncture, the most unlikely of all the men present made a spiritual appeal. Benjamin Franklin, the eldest delegate, and an agnostic on the issue of the deity of Jesus, made a profound speech. He reminded the delegates that in the War for Independence, the Congress continually prayed for divine protection.

> Our prayers, Sir, were heard, and they were graciously answered. All of us who were engaged in the struggle must have observed frequent instances of a superintending Providence in our favor.... And have we now forgotten this powerful Friend?...I have lived, Sir, a long time, and the longer I live, the more convincing proofs I see of this truth—*that God governs in the affairs of men.*

Franklin then noted that if a sparrow cannot fall to the ground without God's notice, how could an empire rise without His aid? The Sacred Writings, he told his fellow delegates, assure us that unless the Lord builds the house, the work will be in vain.

I firmly believe this, and I also believe that without His concurring aid, we shall succeed in this political building no better than the builders of Babel. We shall be divided by our little partial local interests; our projects will be confounded; and we ourselves shall become a reproach and bye word down to future ages....

I therefore beg leave to move that henceforth prayers imploring the assistance of Heaven and its blessings on our deliberations be held in this Assembly every morning before we proceed to business.[22]

Franklin's request for prayers each morning did not pass, but it was not due to impiety. The delegates were embarrassed that they had no funds to hire a chaplain and were concerned that this late call for a chaplain might disclose the problems they were having to a country awaiting the results of their deliberations. But they did request that prayers be offered and sermons be preached on the anniversary of the signing of the Declaration. It was shortly after Franklin's appeal that the deadlock was broken and the Convention concluded its business successfully.

The key was Roger Sherman's compromise proposal for the House of Representatives to be elected according to state population and for the Senate to have an equal representation for each state. This satisfied both the large and small states and avoided the dissolution of the Convention.

Some critics of the Constitution have called it merely a bundle of compromises, using the term compromise in its negative sense. I believe a better perspective is to see it as the high-water mark of unity and union. The delegates found common ground and were, for the most part, gratified with the result. Apparently, that common ground was found throughout the country; enough states ratified the Constitution within the year for the first elections to be held by 1789. Even those who opposed ratification lined up behind the fledgling government once Washington received the unanimous vote of the electors to take the reins as president.

The people of early America could hold a convention and design a new government based on Biblical principles because a Christian consensus dominated the era. They were generally united on certain self-evident truths: that there was a creator God who gave them their rights; that He had absolute standards of right and wrong; that someday every person would have to stand before this God and give an account of his actions; and that heaven and hell were actual places where people would spend eternity. What type of Constitution would emerge from a convention held in modern America?

America's New Basis of Unity and Union

America's Biblical consensus shattered after the 1859 publication of Darwin's *Origin of Species*, which proposed an evolutionary explanation for the origin and development of all life. His explanation began to dominate all academic fields.

Karl Marx then hitched his socialist/communist theories onto Darwin's bandwagon, and the union of both led to a new conception of government. Government became a living organism based upon moral relativism because evolution taught that there were no moral absolutes. This relativism fit perfectly with Marxism, which declared actions "moral" if they furthered the communist cause. In the socialist phase of Marxist thought, government had to take total control of people's lives. This occurred in Russia's Bolshevik Revolution in 1917, which became the pattern for countless twentieth-century revolutions.

America did not suffer a communist revolution, but the welfare-state concept that had its origins in evolutionary-socialistic Progressivism, its first fruits in Franklin Roosevelt's New Deal, and its major victories in Lyndon Johnson's Great Society, has changed the way Americans think about government's role and responsibilities. A new unity of thought grounded in Marx and Darwin (even though many individuals have no idea they are following these men) has created an entirely different union, one alien to the intentions of America's founders.

This new unity of thought has attacked the voluntary association that is an integral part of Biblical unity and union. Labor unions, with the backing of civil government, have set up closed shops. Unless a person joins the union, he cannot work. One of the strongest manifestations of this is found in the National Education Association (NEA), which is pushing for total control of all education in the country. It promotes the policy that all teachers must belong to the NEA or they cannot teach in the public school system. The NEA would like to control all private education, placing restrictions and "calling the shots" for Christian schools and for those who choose to home school. What happened to diversity?

Education has become compulsory; there are no options until a child is past age sixteen. Christian parents who do not want to comply with state education regulations often are denied liberty of conscience; some have been sent to jail for trying to maintain control over what their children are taught.

The same mentality dominates the abortion battle. Government decrees that the "unalienable Right to Life" no longer exists for the unborn child, and everyone must fall in line with this "law of the land." Christians who protest are dragged off to jail and sometimes physically abused in the process. Force is used to compel compliance, but force is never a good basis for union.

In hundreds of other ways, both small and large, government regulations restrict the voluntary actions of individuals in business dealings. Private property is not as private as it used to be. A man may have to rent a house to a homosexual couple because the law forbids discrimination, even though that man may believe homosexuality is a sin and a spiritual plague on society. One applicant for a job may have lesser qualifications than another applicant, but if he is a member of a government-protected minority, he may get the job anyway so the owner can avoid the threat of a lawsuit. Minorities should not be treated prejudicially, but neither should a person who has the "bad fortune" to be part of a majority. Yet government now dictates how hiring should be done, and quotas often are set up (even though the word quota is rarely used).

The most deceptive part of all this is the manner in which it is carried out. The goals often sound excellent. Few people want to be viewed as racists or as insensitive to the disabled. Yet under the guise of helping others, American society has severely abridged the rights of life, liberty, and the pursuit of happiness, even for those for whom the new laws are written. As study after study has revealed, the welfare state has created an American underclass, dependent on government for its existence, destroying family, education, and personal safety. Those who were supposed to be helped have suffered from the designs of the helpers.[23]

The new American unity and union is modeled on a Biblical precedent. That precedent, however, is not one to admire. It is found in Genesis 11, shortly after the Flood:

Now the whole earth used the same language and the same words. And it came about as they journeyed east, that they found a plain in the land of Shinar and settled there. And they said to one another, "Come, let us make bricks and burn them thoroughly." ... And they said, "Come, let us build for ourselves a city, and a tower whose top will reach into heaven, and let us make for ourselves a name; lest we be scattered abroad over the face of the whole earth." And the Lord came down to see the city and the tower which the sons of men had built. And the Lord said, "Behold, they are one people, and they all have the same language. And this is what they began to do, and now nothing which they purpose to do will be impossible for them. Come, let Us go down and there confuse their language, that they may not understand one another's speech." So the Lord scattered them abroad from there over the face of the whole earth; and they stopped building the city. Therefore its name was called Babel, because there the Lord confused the language of the whole earth; and from there the Lord scattered them abroad over the face of the whole earth.[24]

The Tower of Babel incident illustrates a governmental unity and union opposed to God. The people were united in belief and purpose, but neither was according to God's ways. I find the Lord's comment, "now nothing which they purpose to do will be impossible for them," to be fascinating. Apparently, unity and union is a powerful principle even when it works contrary to God's intentions. God found it necessary to divide them so that they wouldn't come up with further ungodly schemes.

Will the Lord confuse and divide the architects of the modern welfare state? Already the socialist vision has failed in Eastern Europe, but will America recognize in time that it also is following socialist principles? I don't think there will be any significant change unless the

Christians do some uniting of their own. If those who claim the name of Christ will again adhere to a belief in God's principles and move toward His goals for civil government, they can establish a powerful union that might—just might—be strong enough to reverse the tide. But that external union still awaits internal unity.

CHAPTER 6

CHRISTIAN CHARACTER: THE CATALYST

Individuality that does not recognize God's purposes becomes an excuse for eccentricity. Selfish self-government is rebellion. The right to hold property, lacking the stewardship concept, becomes an avenue to greed and materialism. The unity upon which a union is founded may have a selfish orientation, as in the illustration of the Tower of Babel. A catalyst is needed.

A catalyst is something that is put into a formula that initiates change. Christian character is the essential catalytic agent for ensuring that these principles are understood and acted upon according to Biblical standards. Without Christian character, these principles degenerate into humanistic drivel. With Christian character, they become powerful truths that can place individuals, churches, and even civil governments on a solid Biblical foundation.

The Source of Christian Character

There is only one model for Christian character—God Himself. I call Christian character a principle because it is a general truth—the character of God has to permeate the creation in order for the creation to function the way He intended.

Christian character is the development of *God's* character in an individual, through the various trials, decisions, and circumstances of life. The result is a life more closely conformed to the image of Christ, "that He might be," says Paul, "the first-born among many brethren."[1]

The definition of the word character refers to a mark made by cutting, engraving, stamping, or pressing. A typewriter [remember that old machine?] leaves a character by the force of a key hitting the ribbon. A sculptor cuts a block of marble to create something beautiful. That is what God does with His people. He is constantly using the trials of life to chip away the rough edges until the image of Christ begins to appear in that block of stone. The chipping can hurt, but the reward is eternal.

Christian character is first internal; the Spirit of God works on thoughts, attitudes, motives, and emotions. God implants His character and displaces man's sinful habits. Man internalizes the heart and mind of Christ, and the image of Christ becomes visible externally. Paul summarized it best when he told the Corinthians, "You are our letter, written in our hearts, known and read by all men; being manifested that you are a letter of Christ, cared for by us, written not with ink, but with the Spirit of the living God, not on tablets of stone, but on tablets of human hearts."[2] All character begins *within* the individual.

Man's character is to be modeled after God's. What is God's character? The apostle John declares, "Beloved, let us love one another, for love is from God; and everyone who loves is born of God and knows God. The one who does not love does not know God, for God is love."[3]

Love seems a logical place to begin because we know it was the love of God that sent Jesus to suffer and die for man's sins. The word does need some definition, however.

The Biblical concept of love differs from the world's concept. People say they "fall in love." Do they really? If what they mean by "love" is that their heart beats faster and they have an emotional attachment to another person, they are not in agreement with the Biblical definition. While there may be emotion connected with love, it is not the focus. The Greek word used when speaking of God's love—agape—does not emphasize emotion. The Greek lexicon does include affection as part of the definition, but goes on to say that agape means goodwill or benevolence. Noah Webster's original 1828 dictionary defines benevolence as "the disposition to do good;... kindness;... the love of mankind, accompanied with a desire to promote their happiness." This describes God's love.

The apostle Paul tells us how this type of love can be recognized when he explains,

> Love is patient, love is kind, and is not jealous; love does not brag and is not arrogant, does not act unbecomingly; it does not seek its own, is not provoked, does not take into account a wrong suffered, does not rejoice in unrighteousness, but rejoices with the truth; bears all things, believes all things, hopes all things, endures all things.[4]

Love is the absence of selfishness. It is a matter of choice, a deliberate decision to do the best for others. God chooses love at all times. His call to us is to choose to love also, even when our feelings may not prompt us to do so. When the Bible says that God is love, it is not talking about an involuntary part of His nature. If God did not choose love, what meaning could be attached to the idea that God loves us? Where is the value in something that is not a choice? For His love (or ours) to be meaningful, it must be voluntary and require a choice.

Love is a matter of the will, not the emotions. God commands man to love, yet no one can command an emotion into existence. We are told to love our enemies.[5] God demonstrated love in that while we were yet sinners, or enemies, Jesus died for us.[6] Is this a matter of the emotions? Does anyone feel an emotional "love" for enemies? Emotions would lead us in the opposite direction. This shows how vital it is that we recognize love as a choice.

Jesus, when asked about the greatest commandment, replied,

> "You shall *love* the Lord your God with all your heart, and with all your soul, and with all your mind." This is the great and foremost commandment. The second is like it, "You shall *love* your neighbor as yourself." On these two commandments depend the whole Law and the Prophets.[7]

Again we see that love is a command; therefore it is a matter of obedience (choice) for man.

Many other character traits stem from love. Righteousness means dealing rightly, fairly, or justly. It means treating each person impartially, according to what he deserves. God is righteous. Paul states, "For there is no partiality with God."[8] And God demands righteousness from us in our responses to Him and to others.

Mercy, the tendency to be lenient toward the unworthy, is another aspect of love. God is "rich in mercy, because of His great love with which He loved us."[9] It is difficult to be righteous and merciful at the same time. Finney says, "Mercy can never manifest itself except in a manner and upon conditions that do not set aside justice and wisdom."[10] When Jesus died on the cross, He upheld the value of God's law and the penalty of the law, allowing God to show mercy to those who had been lawbreakers, provided they repent of their sins, receive His forgiveness, and continue in His love. He found a way to exercise mercy without destroying righteousness.

Truthfulness is based on love. To be truthful is to state reality at all times, to be free from falsehood and deception. It is never loving to be untruthful, even when it seems like it might be best to engage in a "white lie." Jesus said of the Father, "Thy word is *truth*."[11] Of Himself he declared, "I am the way, and the *truth*, and the life."[12] Of the Holy Spirit, He claimed, "But when He, the Spirit of *truth*, comes, He will guide you into all the *truth*."[13] Paul instructs Christians to speak the truth in love and warns them to lay aside falsehood and "speak truth, each one of you, with his neighbor, for we are members of one another."[14] God's love requires truthfulness.

Humility is part of love. It is freedom from arrogance and pride. Paul's definition of love in I Corinthians 13 excludes arrogance. God is not proud and does not brag. When He tells man to worship him, He has that right because He is the essence of love. Humility is total submission to the will of God and recognition that "apart from Me [Jesus] you can do nothing."[15] The apostle James warns, "God is opposed to the proud, but gives grace to the humble.... Humble yourselves in the presence of the Lord, and He will exalt you."[16] This passage makes it clear that humility is a *choice*.

If love is God's first great attribute, faithfulness is His second. Faithfulness is His promise that He always will maintain His choice of love. He always has loved, He continues to love, and He always will love. As the prophet Malachi told the Jews who returned from exile, "For I, the Lord, do not change; therefore you, O sons of Jacob, are not consumed."[17] James promises, "Every good thing bestowed and every perfect gift is from above, coming down from the Father of lights, with whom there is no variation, or shifting shadow."[18] The writer of Hebrews states, "Jesus Christ is the same yesterday and today and forever."[19] God's moral character, expressed as simply as possible, is:

LOVE + FAITHFULNESS = HOLINESS

Holiness is unclear to some people, but it is merely walking in God's love and remaining faithful to that love. The apostle Peter is not being unreasonable when he says, "But like the Holy One who called you, be holy yourselves also in all your behavior; because it is written, 'You shall be holy, for I am holy.'"[20] He is simply saying that God wants men to choose the best for His kingdom and for others and to continue to do so for the rest of their lives.

Christian Character and Civil Government

Scriptures linking character and government abound. The book of Proverbs offers a number of mini-lessons on the character needed by those who govern. "It is an abomination for kings to commit wickedness, for a throne is established on righteousness," declares Solomon.[21] Character in government is also the subject when he says, "Loyalty and truth preserve the king, and he upholds his throne by righteousness."[22] Another proverb deals with harsh treatment and greed in government: "A leader who is a great oppressor lacks understanding, but he who hates unjust gain will prolong his days."[23] And the character of the governor will have an impact on the governed: "When the righteous increase, the people rejoice, but when a wicked man rules, people groan....The king gives stability to the land by justice, but a man who takes bribes overthrows it."[24]

Even proverbs that do not mention civil government directly have instruction applicable to civil government:

> To show partiality in judgment is not good. He who says to the wicked, "You are righteous," peoples will curse him, nations will abhor him; but to those who rebuke the wicked will be delight, and a good blessing will come upon them.[25]

The prophets spoke out constantly against evil government. The number of passages in the prophetic books decrying evil rulers is so numerous that it would be redundant to quote them all. A representative passage from Isaiah states: "Woe to those who enact evil statutes, and to those who constantly record unjust decisions, so as to deprive the needy of justice, and rob the poor of My people of their rights, in order that widows may be their spoil, and that they may plunder the orphans."[26]

Instructions on character in government began when God first set up a human government with the nation of Israel. When Moses tried to govern by himself, his father-in-law gave him sound advice: "You shall select out of all the people able men who fear God, men of truth, those who hate dishonest gain; and you shall place these over them, as leaders of thousands, of hundreds, of fifties and of tens."[27]

Note the qualifications for these civil leaders: they were to be able men who feared God, who were devoted to telling the truth, and who abhorred dishonesty and greed. Ability, by itself, was not enough. A man may have the necessary skills to hold an office, but he also must have the necessary character.

When Moses later recounted this episode, he reminded the Israelites of the instructions he gave to these leaders:

> Then I charged your judges at that time, saying, "Hear the cases between your fellow countrymen, and judge righteously between a man and his fellow countryman, or the alien who is with him. You shall not show partiality in judgment; you shall hear the small and the great alike. You shall not fear man, for the judgment is God's."[28]

They were to judge impartially. They also were not to fear man, but were to judge with the knowledge that they were carrying out God's will, and that they would have to answer to Him ultimately.

Leviticus, the book that catalogs all the laws by which the people of Israel were to live, instructs leaders, "You shall do no injustice in judgment; you shall not be partial to the poor nor defer to the great, but you are to judge your neighbor fairly."[29] God spells out His desire for impartiality emphatically. One might expect a warning against favors for the mighty or wealthy, but God's Word is balanced; He also includes a warning against favoritism toward the poor. Poverty does not automatically make one more spiritual or more acceptable to God; instead, He looks at the heart. Those who have leadership responsibility must reflect God's character in this.

Greater insight as to why civil rulers must be above reproach is given in Deuteronomy:

> You shall not distort justice; you shall not be partial, and you shall not take a bribe, for a bribe blinds the eyes of the wise and perverts the words of the righteous. Justice, and only justice, you shall pursue, that

you may live and possess the land which the Lord your God is giving you.[30]

A man may start out righteous, but if he gives in to bribery, he will become spiritually blind and perverted. Notice the emphatic nature of the phrase, "Justice, and only justice, you shall pursue." The Lord seems to be quite single-minded on this issue. This stresses the importance of putting justice first in civil government.

When Moses spoke to the people about their probable apostasy at some future time and the desire they would have for a king, he warned about the dangers of giving someone so much authority. He gave instructions on acceptable behavior for a king:

> He shall not multiply horses for himself.... Neither shall he multiply wives for himself, lest his heart turn away; nor shall he greatly increase silver and gold for himself.

> Now it shall come about when he sits on the throne of his kingdom, he shall write for himself a copy of this law on a scroll in the presence of the Levitical priests. And it shall be with him, and he shall read it all the days of his life, that he may learn to fear the Lord his God, by carefully observing all the words of this law and these statutes, that his heart may not be lifted up above his countrymen and that he may not turn aside from the commandment, to the right or the left.[31]

First is a warning against material possessions; a focus on external riches could turn his heart away from God and his duties. He is instructed instead to immerse himself in an understanding of God's laws, in the hope that constant attention to God's ways will keep him humble and righteous. This is the type of ruler King David extolled when he penned these words:

> The God of Israel said,
> The Rock of Israel spoke to me,
> "He who rules over men righteously,
> Who rules in the fear of God,
> Is as the light of the morning when the sun rises,
> A morning without clouds,
> When the tender grass springs out of the earth,
> Through sunshine after rain."[32]

Did these instructions on righteous government ever show fruit in Israel? Occasionally rulers were obedient to what God expected of them. When the prophet and judge Samuel stepped down from his civil position, he asked the people,

> "Whose ox have I taken, or whose donkey have I taken, or whom have I defrauded? Whom have I oppressed, or from whose hand have I taken a bribe to blind my eyes with it? I will restore it to you." And they said, "You have not defrauded us, or oppressed us, or taken anything from any man's hand." And he said to them, "The Lord is witness against you, and His anointed this day that you have found nothing in my hand." And they said, "He is witness."[33]

What a powerful testimony of character! Samuel had maintained a clear conscience before both God and man and could now walk away from his civil responsibilities without a regret of any kind. How many modern politicians can say the same?

David sometimes sinned when he was king. When he committed adultery and then had the woman's husband killed by putting him in the front of the battle, God's judgment fell. Another time, puffed up with pride, he had a census taken to know the extent of his empire. God disciplined him for that also.

Yet David showed complete humility and a repentant spirit when confronted by the truth and God's discipline. The Bible calls him "a man after His [God's] own heart."[34] Although this man after God's heart lost his way a few times, he kept returning to the heart and character of God.

When the Queen of Sheba visited King Solomon, she was impressed not just with his riches, but with his character:

> It was a true report which I heard in my own land about your words and your wisdom. Nevertheless I did not believe the reports, until I came and my eyes had seen it. And behold, the half was not told me. You exceed in wisdom and prosperity the report which I heard. How blessed are your men, how blessed are these your servants who stand before you continually and hear your wisdom. Blessed be the Lord your God who delighted in you to set you on the throne of Israel; because the Lord loved Israel forever, therefore He made you king, to do justice and righteousness.[35]

This testimony makes Solomon's later apostasy all the more tragic. A civil ruler who had taken on the character of God threw it all away when his many wives led him into idol worship.

After Israel divided into two kingdoms—Israel and Judah—occasionally there was a king of Judah who obeyed God. King Asa "put away the male cult prostitutes from the land, and removed all the idols which his fathers had made." He also removed his mother from her position as queen mother "because she had made a horrid image as an Asherah; and Asa cut down her horrid image and burned it at the brook Kidron." Further, he "commanded Judah to seek the Lord God of their fathers and to observe the law and the commandment."[36]

Then there was Jehoshaphat, another king of Judah, of whom the Scripture says:

> The Lord was with Jehoshaphat because in his early years he walked in the ways his father David had followed. He did not consult the Baals but sought the God of his father and followed his commands rather than the practices of Israel....His heart was devoted to the ways of the Lord; furthermore, he removed the high places and the Asherah poles from Judah.[37]

Jehoshaphat also reminded the judges of Judah that when they rendered judgment, they were not doing it for man, but for the Lord. He warned: "Now then let the fear of the Lord be upon you; be very careful what you do, for the Lord our God will have no part in unrighteousness, or partiality, or the taking of a bribe."[38] Clearly, the king was concerned about the character of his kingdom.

King Hezekiah had a strong testimony. Not only did he remove idols from the land, but he destroyed the bronze serpent that Moses had made when the Israelites were in the wilderness. It had become an object of worship rather than a reminder of God's healing. Hezekiah "trusted in the Lord, the God of Israel; so that after him there was none like him among all the kings of Judah, nor among those who were before him."[39]

Another Jewish ruler who ruled in the fear of God did so outside Judah. Daniel, who was taken prisoner during the Babylonian Captivity, rose to prominence in that kingdom. He also served in the Persian Empire and was renowned for his character:

> Then this Daniel began distinguishing himself among the commissioners and satraps because he possessed

an extraordinary spirit, and the king planned to appoint him over the entire kingdom. Then the commissioners and satraps began trying to find a ground of accusation against Daniel in regard to government affairs; *but they could find no ground of accusation or evidence of corruption, inasmuch as he was faithful, and no negligence or corruption was to be found in him.*[40]

Jealous men tried to find fault with Daniel, but there was no fault to be found. Daniel had the character of God.

Examples of evil character are easier to find. Ahab and Jezebel, king and queen of Israel in the days of Elijah the prophet, set a standard for evil. Scripture states, "Surely there was no one like Ahab who sold himself to do evil in the sight of the Lord, because Jezebel his wife incited him."[41] They had a man put to death simply because he wouldn't sell them his vineyard. Both died for that act as a direct result of God's judgment.[42]

Most of the kings were similar to Ahab. God sent prophets to warn them, but they rarely listened. Finally the prophecy of the prophet Micah was fulfilled:

Now hear this, heads of the house of Jacob
And rulers of the house of Israel,
Who abhor justice
And twist everything that is straight,
Who build Zion with bloodshed
And Jerusalem with violent injustice.
Her leaders pronounce a judgment for a bribe,
Her priests instruct for a price,
And her prophets divine for money.
Yet they lean on the Lord saying,
"Is not the Lord in our midst?
Calamity will not come upon us."
Therefore, on account of you,
Zion will be plowed as a field,
Jerusalem will become a heap of ruins,

And the mountain of the temple will become high places of a forest.[43]

The rulers of Judea did not improve in New Testament times. Herod the Great, upon hearing of the birth of the Messiah, was so upset for the future of his throne that he had all male children in the Bethlehem area two years old and younger put to death.[44] Herod Antipas beheaded John the Baptist.[45] Herod Agrippa executed the apostle James. He attempted the same with Peter, but God miraculously freed him. Agrippa himself, according to the book of Acts, was struck down by God for his arrogance:

> And on an appointed day Herod, having put on his royal apparel, took his seat on the rostrum and began delivering an address to them. And the people kept crying out, "The voice of a god and not of a man!" And immediately an angel of the Lord struck him because he did not give God the glory, and he was eaten by worms and died.[46]

All these Judean civil rulers were under the authority of Rome. Pontius Pilate, the Roman procurator for Judea, holds a singular place in human history as the man who sentenced Jesus to crucifixion. Pilate knew he was sentencing an innocent man, but feared for his own position when the Jews threatened to tell Caesar that he had let a rival to the throne live. Although he washed his hands of the affair, he could not wash his conscience. Pilate's act was one of moral cowardice. As a civil ruler, he called good evil and evil good. His deed is now the model for unrighteous government.

Christian Character and American Government

> If we abide by the principles taught in the Bible, our
> country will go on prospering; but if we and our pos-
> terity neglect its instructions and authority, no man
> can tell how sudden a catastrophe may overwhelm us
> and bury all our glory in profound obscurity.[47]

Thus spoke Daniel Webster, who served as a congressman,
senator, and secretary of state. He saw the Bible as foundational to the success of the American republic; not just
the Bible in the abstract, but an adherence to the principles taught in the Bible—men taking on the character
of God.

Webster was not alone in this belief. Early Americans,
grounded in Biblical tradition, never thought that good
government could be separated from Christian character.
Political scientists Charles S. Hyneman and Donald S.
Lutz painstakingly researched every piece of American
political writing between 1760 and 1805. One of their
conclusions, after completing the research, was: "The
importance of public virtue for a self-governing people,
and the importance of religion for public virtue, were
constant themes during the founding era."[48] Further, they
stated:

> Few Americans today realize that the revolutionary
> war was fought as much to preserve American virtue
> as it was to secure economic independence. Americans,
> as well as Europeans, tended to view Americans as
> embodying the sturdy traits of the traditional English
> yeoman—frugality, industriousness, temperance, sim-
> plicity, openness, and virility. They viewed England, on
> the other hand, as the prototype of a corrupt society
> characterized by luxury, venality, effete cowardice, and
> a love of refinement and distinction.... Breaking with

English control thus preserved the basis of American liberty, its pristine virtues, and provided immediate political liberty.[49]

The emphasis on character existed from the very beginning of the American colonies. When the Pilgrims first arrived, character was essential to their survival. William Bradford served as governor of the colony for thirty-five years. Elections were annual and the only times Bradford was not elected were when he chose not to place his name in nomination for the office. That is a testimony to the trust the people placed in him.

Setting up the Pilgrims' Plymouth colony was a struggle, and a test of their character. As Bradford relates:

> In these arduous and difficult beginnings, discontent and murmuring arose amongst some, and mutinous speech and bearing in others; but they were soon quelled and overcome by the wisdom, patience, and just and equal administration of things by the Governor [John Carver at this time] and the better part, who held faithfully together in the main.[50]

During their first winter, diseases took a heavy toll, resulting in the death of approximately half of the original settlers. Six or seven healthy people took care of all the rest, "who, to their great commendation be it spoken, spared no pains night or day," Bradford remembers, "but with great toil and at the risk of their own health,... did all the homely and necessary services for them which dainty and queasy stomachs cannot endure to hear mentioned." They did all this "willingly and cheerfully, without the least grudging, showing their love to the friends and brethren; a rare example and worthy to be remembered."[51]

Bradford contrasts the Pilgrims' character with that of the sailors on the Mayflower. The diseases hit them also but "amongst the sailors there was quite a different bearing." They deserted one another, "saying they would not risk their lives for the sick among them, lest they should be infected by coming to help them in their cabins; if they died, let them die!" One of the sick men made out a will giving all his possessions to another seaman if he would only take care of him until he died. "So his companion went and got a little spice and prepared some food once or twice," Bradford recounts. But "when he did not die as soon as expected, he ... swore the rogue would cheat him of his inheritance; he would see him choke before he prepared him any more food; and so the poor fellow died before morning."[52]

Why did the Pilgrims display such admirable character while the sailors exhibited the opposite? The most obvious reason is their Biblical beliefs.

John Winthrop, first governor of Massachusetts Bay, proclaimed the need for Christian character for his colony to succeed. On the voyage to America, Winthrop preached a sermon to his fellow passengers, telling them what God expected of them as a people—expectations of a certain type of character:

> But if we ... shall fall to embrace this present world and prosecute our carnal intentions, seeking great things for ourselves and our posterity, the Lord will surely break out in wrath against us, be revenged of such a perjured people, and make us know the price of the breach of such a covenant.

That was the warning; next came the exhortation to reproduce the character of God:

Now the only way to avoid this shipwreck, and to provide for our posterity, is to follow the counsel of Micah, to do justly, to love mercy, to walk humbly with our God. For this end, we must be knit together in this work as one man. We must entertain each other in brotherly affection, we must be willing to abridge ourselves of our superfluities, for the supply of others' necessities. We must uphold a familiar commerce together in all meekness, gentleness, patience, and liberality. We must delight in each other, make others' conditions our own, rejoice together, mourn together, labor and suffer together.... So shall we keep the unity of the spirit in the bond of peace.

Winthrop followed this exhortation with the most famous lines of his sermon:

For we must consider that we shall be as a city upon a hill. The eyes of all people are upon us, so that if we deal falsely with our God in this work we have undertaken, and so cause him to withdraw his present help from us, we shall be made a story and a by-word through the world. We shall open the mouths of enemies to speak evil of the ways of God, and all professors [of Christianity] for God's sake. We shall shame the faces of many of God's worthy servants, and cause their prayers to be turned into curses upon us till we be consumed out of the good land whither we are agoing.[53]

Winthrop lived his words. When the settlers arrived in Massachusetts in 1630, they suffered in much the same way as Plymouth had ten years earlier. Food was scarce, disease prevailed, and even Winthrop's own son drowned a few days after arrival. Yet Winthrop remained faithful. He wrote to his wife back in England, "Yet for all these things (I prayse my God) I am not discouraged, nor doe I see cause to repent, or dispaire of those good dayes heere, which will make amends for all."[54]

Winthrop took responsibility for gathering food, dealing with the Indians personally. When the colony was in its deepest crisis, he paid for supplies for everyone out of his own family funds. Eleven servants whom he considered part of his family died. Another letter to his wife reveals the character that sustained him: "I like so well to be heer, as I doe not repent my comminge: and if I were to come againe, I would not have altered my course, though I had forseene all these Afflictions: I never fared better in my life, never slept better, never had more content of minde."[55]

The character that preserved the Pilgrims and the Puritans carried over to the eighteenth century. The Founding Fathers were brought up in church and in a Biblical culture. Their concern for Christian character in government is well documented.

Samuel Adams's character has received considerable scrutiny. Early chroniclers of American history recognized his Puritanism. His concern for strict morals led some people to judge him as too stern, yet as a contemporary wrote, "No individual of his day had so much the feelings of the ancient puritans."[56] Early twentieth-century historians castigated Adams. One commented, "He taught his dog Queue to bite every Red Coat he saw, and took little children to the Commons to teach them to hate British soldiers."[57] Fortunately, the historiographical tide has turned, and Adams is now being treated more sympathetically.

Evidence is strong that Samuel Adams was a Christian and that he sought to establish Christian character in government. On that particular subject he remarked:

A general dissolution of principles and manners will more surely overthrow the liberties of America than the whole force of the common enemy. While the people are virtuous they cannot be subdued; but when once they lose their virtue they will be ready to surrender their liberties to the first external or internal invader.... If virtue and knowledge are diffused among the people, they will never be enslaved. This will be their great security.[58]

In 1772 Adams wrote "The Rights of the Colonists as Men, Christians, and Subjects." In it he acknowledged every principle covered thus far in this book: the right to life [individuality], liberty [self-government], property, and voluntary consent [unity and union]. He also stated that "every man living in or out of a state of civil society has a right peaceably and quietly to worship God according to the dictates of his conscience." He maintained that all of man's civil laws must be based on "the eternal and immutable laws of God and nature." And he took issue with the British government's judgment of American character: "The Colonists have been branded with the odious names of traitors and rebels only for complaining of their grievances. How long such treatment will or ought to be borne, is submitted.[59]

It was Adams the Congregationalist who, at the Continental Congress, nominated an Episcopalian clergyman to give the opening prayer, declaring that he "could hear a prayer from a gentleman of piety and virtue, who was at the same time a friend to his country."[60]

Neither was Adams the rabble-rouser depicted in some histories. As historian Pauline Maier notes:

He never justified force as a first response to oppression.... He condemned the attack on the homes of Thomas Hutchinson and others on August 26, 1765, as a transaction of "a truly *mobbish* Nature." There is no evidence that he prompted the Boston Massacre riot, although he served thereafter as spokesman for the town in demanding that troops be removed from Boston. Adams is said to have signaled the Boston Tea Party, and, although his precise role on December 16, 1773, is disputable, the words attributed to him in the final "Tea Meeting" are in perfect accord with his philosophy: "This meeting can do nothing further to save this country." In effect, all peaceful means of preventing payment of the tea duty, and accepting all it implied, had been exhausted. Only then was the destruction of property justified.[61]

Personal letters are important in determining the character of a man. In 1780 Adams wrote to his daughter to "carefully fulfill the various Duties of Life, from a Principle of Obedience to your heavenly Father." He also counseled her in her pursuit of "the Path of Wisdom and Virtue" to keep in mind that she should do so not to please him, but God. "You know you cannot gratify me so much, as by seeking most earnestly, the Favor of Him who made & supports you—who will supply you with whatever his infinite Wisdom sees best for you in this World, and above all," he concluded, "who has given us his Son to purchase for us the Reward of Eternal Life."[62]

To his future son-in-law Adams gave advice on married life, focusing on character qualities:

> When the married Couple strictly observe the great Rules of Honor & Justice towards each other, Differences, if any happen, between them, must proceed from small & trifling Circumstances....I could dwell on the Importance of Piety & Religion, of Industry & Frugality, of Prudence, Economy, Regularity & an even Government, all which are essential to the Well being of a Family.... I cannot however help repeating Piety,

because I think it indispensable. Religion in a Family is at once its brightest Ornament & its best Security.[63]

He wrote his wife about the importance of character in government:

It is the Duty of every one to use his utmost Exertions in promoting the Cause of Liberty & Virtue; and having so done, if his Country thinks proper to call others to the arduous Task, he ought chearfully to acquiesce, and to console himself with the Contemplations of an honest Man in private Life.... You are Witness that I have not raisd a Fortune in the Service of my Country....If my Mind has ever been tinctured with Envy, the Rich and the Great have not been its objects. If I have been vain, Popularity, tho' I had as much of it as any Man ought to have, is not the Phantome I have pursued....

I will trust in that all gracious Being, who, in his own good Way, has provided us with Food and Raiment; and having spent the greatest Part of my Life in Publick Cares, like the weary Traveller, fatigud with the Journey of the Day, I can rest with you in a Cottage.[64]

Government servants, according to Adams, have a trust from the people who elect them. If the people choose someone else, a good servant retires from the public arena cheerfully and devotes himself to private life. In the twenty-first century, an era when government has become a career rather than a public service, such an attitude as Adams's is rare.

Samuel's cousin, John Adams, America's second president, also had some choice comments about character and government.

We have no government armed with power capable of contending with human passions unbridled by morality and religion. Avarice, ambition, revenge, or gallantry, would break the strongest cords of our Constitution as a whale goes through a net. Our Constitution was made only for a moral and religious people. It is wholly inadequate for the government of any other.[65]

Adams saw that external government, by itself, was insufficient for stability. All government begins with the self, and the self must be remade into the character of God.

Adams further remarked, "Statesmen ... may plan and speculate for liberty, but it is religion and morality alone, which can establish the principles upon which freedom can securely stand. The only foundation of a free constitution is pure virtue."[66] And what is the source of this virtue? "The Christian religion is, above all the religions that ever prevailed or existed in ancient or modern times, the religion of wisdom, virtue, equity, and humanity."[67]

Adams believed that the principles of government "are as easily destroyed, as human Nature is corrupted." Republican government could be supported only "by pure Religion or Austere Morals." He disagreed with the modern American belief that it does not matter what kind of personal life an elected official leads: "Public Virtue cannot exist in a Nation without private, and public virtue is the only Foundation of Republics."[68]

George Washington, like Samuel Adams, has been the subject of intense scrutiny regarding his beliefs and character. Some allege that Washington was not active in a church. This is untrue. I had the opportunity to visit Pohick Episcopal Church, located near Fort Belvoir, while I lived in the Virginia suburbs of Washington, D.C. Pohick served as Washington's home church. He was a vestryman in the church, his attendance disrupted only by the American Revolution and his two terms as president.[69]

The Freemasons claim Washington as one of their own, and this bothers many Christians who know that Masonry is allied to the occult. Yet many colonial Americans joined Masonic lodges purely for social or business contacts, unaware of the discrepancies with Biblical faith. Washington, although officially a Mason, wrote in a 1797 letter that he had not attended a Masonic meeting more than once or twice in the preceding thirty years. This does *not* indicate devotion to the Masonic faith.[70]

Washington's public statements reveal a reliance on God and a concern for character. When he took command of the Continental Army in 1775, the first command he issued was as follows:

> The General most earnestly requires and expects a due observance of those articles of war established for the government of the army, which forbid profane cursing, swearing, and drunkenness. And in like manner he requires and expects of all officers and soldiers, not engaged in actual duty, a punctual attendance on Divine service, to implore the blessing of Heaven upon the means used for our safety and defense.[71]

When Washington resigned from the army eight years later, he commented that he had taken the position because he felt he had "the patronage of Heaven" and "the interposition of Providence" to bring the war to a successful conclusion. He then commended the interests of America "to the protection of Almighty God, and those who have the superintendence of them to His holy keeping."[72]

Upon his election to the presidency in 1789, the new president acknowledged God's oversight of the nation:

> It would be peculiarly improper to omit, in this first official act, my fervent supplications to that Almighty Being who rules over the universe, who presides in the councils of nations and whose providential aids can

supply every human defect.... No people can be bound to acknowledge and adore the Invisible Hand which conducts the affairs of men more than the people of the United States. Every step by which they have advanced to the character of an independent nation seems to have been distinguished by some token of providential agency;... We ought to be no less persuaded that the propitious smiles of Heaven can never be expected on a nation that disregards the eternal rules of order and right which Heaven itself has ordained.[73]

As president, Washington set a precedent by issuing proclamations for days of prayer and thanksgiving. Upon leaving office, his Farewell Address did not neglect to mention character:

Of all the dispositions and habits which lead to political prosperity, Religion and Morality are indispensable supports. In vain would that man claim the tribute of Patriotism, who should labor to subvert these great pillars of human happiness, these firmest props of the duties of Men and Citizens.... Let it simply be asked, where is the security for property, for reputation, for life, if the sense of religious obligation desert the oaths which are the instrument of investigation in Courts of Justice? And let us with caution indulge the supposition that morality can be maintained without religion.... Reason and experience both forbid us to expect that national morality can prevail in exclusion of religious principle.

It is substantially true that virtue or morality is a necessary spring of popular government.... Who, that is a sincere friend to it, can look with indifference upon attempts to shake the foundation of the fabric?[74]

Washington calls religion and morality "indispensable" for government. Without them there would be no security for life or property because there would be no basis for justice. Any attempt to set up a morality without divine authority would be a disaster.

The break with Britain was as much about character as self-government and property. The Declaration of Independence speaks of the prudence and patience of the colonies contrasted with the "long train of abuses and usurpations" perpetrated by the king. George III sought "to reduce them under absolute despotism" and establish "an absolute Tyranny over these States." A list of specific abuses concludes: "A Prince, whose character is thus marked by every act which may define a Tyrant, is unfit to be the ruler of a free People." Character is paramount in the concluding sentence: "And for the support of this Declaration, with a firm reliance on the Protection of Divine Providence, we mutually pledge to each other our Lives, our Fortunes and our sacred Honor."

The men who signed this document became marked. Their lives, families, and property became targets for the British, who wished to teach these traitors a lesson. They suffered tremendous loss during the prosecution of the war, but they had pledged to continue—it was a matter of faithfulness, a matter of character.

Eighty-seven years later, in the midst of an awful war between the states, when Christian character seemed scarce, another president, in emulation of Washington, proclaimed a national day of prayer and fasting. In his proclamation, Abraham Lincoln recognized the need for repentance and humility when he said,

> It is the duty of nations as well as of men, to own their dependence upon the overruling power of God, to confess their sins and transgressions, in humble sorrow, yet with assured hope that genuine repentance will lead to mercy and pardon; and to recognize the sublime truth, announced in the Holy Scriptures and proven by

all history, that those nations only are blessed whose God is the Lord.

Lincoln said that the war had come upon America for one reason:

> We have forgotten God. We have forgotten the gracious hand which has preserved us in peace, and multiplied and enriched and strengthened us; and we have vainly imagined, in the deceitfulness of our hearts, that all these blessings were produced by some superior wisdom and virtue of our own. Intoxicated with unbroken success, we have become too self-sufficient to feel the necessity of redeeming and preserving grace, too proud to pray to the God that made us!

> It behooves us then to humble ourselves before the offended Power, to confess our national sins and to pray for clemency and forgiveness.[75]

Since Lincoln's time America has turned away from God and Christian character in an unprecedented way. Abortion is considered a legal "right." Homosexuality is given politically protected status, homosexual congressmen are reelected by large margins, and "same-sex marriage" is threatening to destroy Biblical marriage as a societal institution. Dan Quayle, when he was vice-president, decried the breakup of the family and the growing acceptance of illegitimate births; he was ridiculed for doing so. John F. Kennedy had an obsession with illicit sexual relationships and had ties to organized crime. Richard Nixon resigned in disgrace after obstructing a federal investigation. Bill Clinton was impeached by the House of Representatives for perjury and obstruction of justice and put on trial in the Senate. He was acquitted only because no one in his own party would vote for removal from office.

We are a nation morally adrift. We are concerned about AIDS sufferers and single mothers, but we do not talk about the sinful actions that created most of the problems. That would be "judgmental." The idea of sin has disappeared almost completely, relegated to "fringe religious groups" who have not yet entered the enlightened world of twenty-first-century moral relativism. God has a remedy, enunciated in II Chronicles 7:14:

> If My people who are called by My name humble themselves and pray, and seek My face and turn from their wicked ways, then I will hear from heaven, will forgive their sin, and will heal their land.

The only answer to the myriad problems plaguing America today is to return to God and His character. Humility and repentance are the keys. LOVE + FAITHFULNESS = HOLINESS.

CHAPTER 7

BIBLICAL FORM OFGOVERNMENT: GOD WANTS KINGS?

G overnment, as stated previously, is merely control and direction. Civil government is control and direction of a community. It is not evil, but a God-ordained institution. Yet, as with every gift of God, it can be abused. How does the Lord want Christians to view civil government?

Why Civil Government?

"Submit yourselves for the Lord's sake to every human institution," writes the apostle Peter, "whether to a king as the one in authority, or to governors as sent by him for the punishment of evildoers and the praise of those who do right."[1]

Paul, in his first letter to Timothy, gives another insight into the purpose of government: "First of all, then, I urge that entreaties and prayers, petitions and thanksgivings, be made on behalf of all men, for kings and all who are in authority, in order that we may lead a tranquil and quiet life in all godliness and dignity."[2] In other words, civil government is to establish domestic peace. It is to order the community so that people can go about their business undisturbed.

In Romans 13 Paul instructs believers to obey governing authorities because God establishes them. Government has a divine origin. Anyone who resists authority, according to Paul, "has opposed the ordinance of God; and they who have opposed will receive condemnation upon themselves."[3]

He repeats the purpose found in Peter's letter: "For it is a minister of God to you for good," he emphasizes. "But if you do what is evil, be afraid; for it does not bear the sword for nothing; for it is a minister of God, an avenger who brings wrath upon the one who practices evil."[4] Paul reminds his readers that since they understand the purpose of government, they are to obey, not just because they may be punished if they don't, but because their consciences instruct them to be obedient.

From these Scriptures, it seems that the two main reasons for civil government are to punish evildoers and to protect citizens. These reasons give Biblical sanction to a police force to keep domestic peace, a military force for repelling an invasion, a legislature to pass just laws, and courts to deal with both civil and criminal cases. It also follows that government is not fulfilling its God-ordained purposes when evildoers go unpunished, when those who do good things *are* punished, or when the lives and property of its citizens are endangered, either by other people or by the government itself.

Romans 13 is not a call to unthinking obedience to *any* type of government. Civil government should be serving God. So what is the Christian's response if the government is doing the opposite of its God-intended purposes? Again, Scripture gives the answer.

When the Hebrews were slaves in Egypt and grew strong enough to alarm Pharaoh, he passed an edict requiring Hebrew midwives to kill all newborn boys. "But the midwives feared God, and did not do as the king of Egypt commanded them, but let the boys live.... So God was good to the midwives, and the people multiplied, and became mighty."[5]

Babylon destroyed Judah and took captives. Some were raised in Babylonian ways and were expected to obey the king's commands. But when King Nebuchadnezzar ordered everyone to bow down to his golden statue, three Hebrew men refused. Enraged, the king had them thrown into a furnace so hot that it killed the men who threw them in. Yet God delivered the Hebrews who had remained faithful to Him. He stood with them in their civil disobedience.[6]

Wise men traveled to Judea to see the newborn king of the Jews. King Herod, jealous of any promise of a Messiah, instructed them to report back to him to tell him where this new king was to be found, but God Himself warned the men in a dream not to return to Herod, and they departed for their own country by another way.[7]

On two occasions officials arrested the apostles for preaching. At their first hearing, Peter and John proclaimed, "Whether it is right in the sight of God to give heed to you rather than to God, you be the judge; for we cannot stop speaking what we have seen and heard."[8] When brought before the rulers a second time, they were even more blunt: "We must obey God rather than men."[9]

Civil government, although established by God, is not the ultimate authority. It is to be obeyed unless it goes against *the* Authority who first gave civil government *its* authority.

Christians live in two kingdoms. They are first citizens of heaven. "The kingdom of God is within you," Jesus taught.[10] When the crowds tried to make Him an earthly king, He withdrew. When Pilate asked if He were a king, he responded, "My kingdom is not of this world."[11] Then when Pilate tried to tell Jesus that he had the authority either to release or crucify Him, Jesus put the proper perspective on the situation when He answered, "You would have no authority over Me, unless it had been given you from above."[12]

Yet Christians also live in this world. They can have an influence on how government operates, helping to keep it within its God-ordained boundaries. That is the essence of what Jesus taught in one portion of the Sermon on the Mount:

> You are the light of the world. A city set on a hill cannot be hidden. Nor do men light a lamp, and put it under the peckmeasure, but on the lampstand; and it gives light to all who are in the house. Let your light shine before men in such a way that they may see your good works, and glorify your Father who is in heaven.[13]

If Christians withdraw their influence from civil government, what guarantees are there that the government will be faithful to Biblical principles?

A Biblical Form of Government Defined

God is interested in the government of the world and is concerned that men follow His laws. He has given guidelines for the form of government best suited to fulfill His purposes.

A *form* is a manner or system, a stated method or practice, or an appropriate arrangement of parts. A Biblical form of government would be a Biblical manner or system of government [control and direction]; a Biblical method or practice of control and direction; an appropriate Biblical arrangement of the parts of government to achieve control and direction. What manner or system, or arrangement of parts, did God ordain?

The first governmental institution established by God was the family. He gave the husband authority over the wife, and children were to obey their parents. Information on civil authority before the Flood is sketchy; it seems that the family, or tribal, structure predominated. The same pattern can be seen post-Flood in Abraham, although kings became predominant.

The first time man attempted centralized government power was the Tower of Babel. We already saw how God reacted to this attempt. When He scattered the people, He decentralized authority.

Specific instructions on civil government began when Moses led the children of Israel toward the Promised Land. First God gave them the Ten Commandments as a basis for all their laws. Then He allowed a certain form of government to be set up.

Moses tried to judge all the people by himself. His father-in-law, Jethro, warned him that he would wear himself out, and that he needed others to share the burden with him. So Moses told the people, "Choose wise and discerning and experienced men from your tribes, and I will appoint them as your heads."[14] After the people of each tribe chose leaders, Moses appointed them "leaders of thousands, and of hundreds, of fifties and of tens, and officers" for their tribes.[15] They were to judge cases at their various levels. If a case at the top level was too difficult to handle, they could bring it to Moses. When they eventually entered the land, they continued this pattern, with Moses' role being taken either by a priest or a judge called specifically by God to serve in that capacity.

Israel in the days of the judges was a federal republic. This assertion may surprise some people, but whenever

power is diffused throughout different levels of government, where each level has its own sphere of authority,
and where the top level does not involve itself with local
governmental affairs unless asked to do so, the structure
is federalism. It is an effective protection against tyranny.
In addition, the people chose their leaders; representation is the key ingredient for what political thinkers have
always called a republic. The system in early Israel was
therefore a federal republic.

The problem with any federal republic is that it calls
for a high degree of self-government. If the people are
unwilling to abide by the law, the structure breaks down.
Those who refuse to be self-governed need a strong
external governor to control them. This was the case
with Israel. The phrase that keeps recurring throughout
the book of Judges is, "In those days there was no king in
Israel; everyone did what was right in his own eyes."[16]

Reading the book of Judges can be discouraging. The
people begin with their hearts right before God, they fall
into rebellion, God allows a foreign enemy to oppress
them, they cry out to God for deliverance, and He sends
a deliverer. For a while they remain true to His law, but
then the cycle repeats: rebellion, oppression, repentance,
deliverance. They never learn. Throughout this sad spectacle, God tries to teach them to be responsible and
accountable, but they keep turning away. Moreover, they
begin looking at the government of other nations and
long to have the same type of government themselves.

The governmental issue came to a head during
Samuel's judgeship. The elders of Israel came to Samuel
and demanded to have a king "like all the nations."[17] This
demand did not please Samuel, and he went before God
to ask for guidance. The Lord's response cut to the core:
"Listen to the voice of the people in regard to all that
they say to you, for they have not rejected you, but they

have rejected Me from being king over them." Under His Lordship, God had given these people a unique form of government, one that allowed them the greatest civil liberty on earth; but because of their rebellion they repudiated God's form and opted instead for a human king. Although this was not God's design for His chosen people, He allowed it because their lack of self-government required a stronger hand in leadership. Evidently their character was so corrupt that self-government would not work: "Like all the deeds which they have done since the day that I brought them up from Egypt even to this day— in that they have forsaken Me and served other gods—so they are doing to you also," He informed Samuel.

Although God allowed them to alter His design, He instructed Samuel to "solemnly warn them and tell them of the procedure of the king who will reign over them." The reason the Lord had not given them a human king was that men in power tend to grow fond of their power. He hoped by describing to His people the way kings typically behave that they might yet turn away from this foolish demand.

Samuel gave the people a grim description of what was in store for them if they got the king they desired. He warned that their king would take their sons to labor in his fields and in his armed forces, and that he would seize their daughters for perfumers, cooks, and bakers. No man's property would be safe because the king would grab the best fields, vineyards, and olive groves. He would take one-tenth of all the people's produce (otherwise known as taxes). Male and female servants would be confiscated, and the best of their flocks and herds. Samuel's final words of warning should have made all sensible people reconsider: "Then you will cry out in that day because of your king whom you have chosen for yourselves, but the Lord will not answer you in that day."

The people of Israel, however, chose to disregard Samuel's warnings. Their response, recorded for the instruction of all generations, was astounding in its foolishness: "No, but there shall be a king over us, that we also may be like all the nations, that our king may judge us and go out before us and fight our battles."

An examination of their response reveals their hearts. First, they were more concerned with being like everybody else than with being a special people of God. This was a rejection of their individuality. It is a desire to be like the world. Second, they wanted the king to take care of them, to make all the decisions and to fight their battles for them. This is an abdication of responsibility and accountability. It is also an illusion—that government somehow will take care of everything and we won't have to worry. In fact, it is when government starts to take care of everything that the real worries begin.

The conclusion is that God did not initiate the establishment of kingship in Israel, nor did He approve of it. He let the people have a king only because they refused to be governed in His way, a way built on the principles of individuality, self-government, property, unity and union, and Christian character.

The New Testament does not have an example of a form of civil government set up by God, but church government can serve as a model for governmental principles in general. What we find is consistency with the Old Testament pattern.

Representation was introduced in Acts 6 when the whole congregation chose seven men to serve as deacons. Although God appointed apostles, they were primarily missionaries, establishing new congregations and then moving on to other places. Paul, in particular, established churches and wrote instructions for them, but the everyday government was in the hands of elders and deacons chosen from the local churches.[18] Acts 6 indicates that congregations were involved in the choice. Church government was local; each church was a self-governing body of believers. Elaborate ecclesiastical hierarchies were a later development without Scriptural warrant—creations of man, not of God.

Thus far, two external aspects of a Biblical form of government have been discussed: representation and federalism. Scripture also recognizes another truth about government—that it has more than one branch. "For the Lord is our judge, the Lord is our lawgiver, the Lord is our king; He will save us," declares Isaiah.[19] These are the three branches of government commonly acknowledged today. Isaiah points out how the Lord functions in all three capacities. He is the judge because He determines right and wrong; He is the lawgiver because He knows what laws are essential for human happiness; and He is the king, or the executive arm of government, the branch that enforces the law.

A Biblical view of human sinfulness would want to separate these powers as much as possible. If one man or a small group of men had the power to make all laws, enforce them, and decide whether they were good laws, tyranny could result. Therefore, a government based on a Biblical understanding of man would recognize this danger and guard against it. If God were ruling in person, there would be no problem, but no man can claim the same degree of love and wisdom that resides in God.

These three external structures—representation, separation of powers, and federalism—are all Biblical protections against the sinfulness of man. Any government that incorporates all three has a better chance of reducing the threat of unprincipled power-seekers. When these three are in operation, we have the closest thing to a Christian form of government possible—a federal republic.

Yet setting up an external structure that is supposed to diffuse power will be futile unless internal Biblical principles are part of a people's beliefs and practices. A nation must believe in individuality, that God created each person for a purpose, that the life of each person is valuable because man is created in the image of God. It must practice self-government and accountability toward property or it will fall like Israel under the judges. Voluntary unity and union must be a component or the civil government will possess enforcement powers far beyond its legitimate functions. Christian character must be considered essential to the proper exercise of government; without unsullied character in government officials, government simply will become the Big Brother that hands out favors in exchange for maintaining the status quo.

The internal and external aspects of a Biblical form of government, therefore, can be listed as follows:

INTERNAL	EXTERNAL
Individuality Self-Government Property Unity and Union Christian Character	Representation Separation of Powers Federalism (different levels of government)

Only a federal republic allows individuality, self-government, property, unity and union, and Christian character to have their full impact on society. Totalitarian systems contradict the first four principles. The systems themselves eventually destroy Christian character because of the corruption that comes from absolute power.

Strong monarchies/dictatorships, socialism/communism, and fascism are all totalitarian. Egalitarian democracy, which attempts to destroy all distinctions between individuals and force equal distribution of property, is also totalitarian through a tyranny of the majority. Minority rights are not protected. If 51 percent of the people believe something should be a law, it will become law even if it tramples on the individuality, self-government, property, and unity and union of the other 49 percent. Only a federal republic gives people the possibility of realizing their individuality by offering the liberty to follow wherever God may lead.

The United States still maintains its original structure. People vote for their representatives, the powers are still technically separated, and state and local governments continue to operate. Yet something has gone awry. The same representatives keep getting elected even though there is almost universal disdain for the national Congress. The judicial power has stepped into the legislative role. And state and local governments are often little more than extensions of the national power, receiving grants and following the regulations issued from on high.

The structure exists. A federal republic is still on the books. Yet it is not functioning as intended. What has gone wrong? The external structure needs the internal Biblical principles for it to operate properly, and those principles have eroded significantly in the last two hundred years. A short history of American government from its Biblical beginnings to the present should make this evident.

America ... In the Beginning

Most history texts consider ancient Greece as the model for American government. Greece, they say, is the source of Western "democratic" institutions. The reality is that Greek government was man-centered, not God-centered. The common conception of the Greek gods was that they were more like corrupt men who had to be bribed so they would not send misery upon the people.

Greek city-states were selfish to the extreme and were unable to form any type of union. Within the cities government sometimes degenerated into mob rule whenever a demagogue could whip up the emotions of the populace. The individual lacked value because he was not a being made in the image of an all-wise god. He was important only in relation to his city. If he offered something of value to the city, he was significant; if he did not, he was unimportant. The Greeks' debased life-style shows the cheapness of human life in the society. Abortion, infanticide, and homosexuality were accepted. Although this may seem similar to modern America, it was not America's foundation.

Rome considered itself the great civilizer. It emphasized the importance of law. Yet law was considered man-made; there was no concept of an eternal law binding upon all men. Civil government granted all rights. If the government grants a right, the government can take it away. When Rome became an empire, representation was not part of its structure. Individuals in conquered provinces might be granted Roman citizenship, but they had no voice in how government operated.

One can critique the Middle Ages for its theology and hierarchical structure, both in church and state, but there was a basic Christian foundation to government. Nearly everyone accepted certain truths: God's law was sovereign; the king was under God's law and civil law; a ruler could hold office only if he took an oath before God to keep the faith; and kingdoms might crumble, but God's law would always continue. Although the structure was not consistent with most of the Biblical principles covered thus far, these beliefs kept the Middle Ages on a Biblical track.

When the Reformation shattered the monopoly of the Catholic Church, the reformers did not repudiate the basic beliefs about government, but they did add to that thought. They made a stronger case for the idea that rights come from God. They emphasized the Old Testament covenant theory of government and developed a theory of resistance to ungodly government. Most of the reformers did not accept the divine-right-of-kings theory, which said that the king had a direct grant from God to rule as he saw fit. If a king broke his covenant relationship with his people by endangering their rights, Christian citizens were duty-bound to disobey.

Reformation thought merged with English tradition as it passed into its American form. Both Englishmen and Americans looked to documents such as the Magna Carta (1215), the Petition of Right (1628), and the English Bill of Rights (1689) as reaffirmations of the Biblical basis for government.[20]

English Common Law also influenced American theories of government. The Common Law rested on traditional unwritten beliefs about right and wrong. A case would come before a judge who would then make a decision after consideration of precedent and traditional beliefs, most of which were founded upon the Bible. This was not pure precedent *divorced* from eternal law, but precedent *united* with eternal law.

The Mayflower Compact, written by the Pilgrims in 1620, was the first American document of Christian self-government. As one author has stated:

> The document represents the application to the affairs of civil government of the philosophy of the church covenant which was the basis of Puritan theology. This theology found in the Scriptures the right of men to associate and covenant to form a church and civil government and to choose their own officers to administer both religious and civil affairs. Each member of the congregation had a vote in the election of officers, and each congregation was considered as independent and autonomous of every other and not subject to the authority of any centralized church hierarchy.[21]

The separatism of the Pilgrims influenced the Puritans of Massachusetts and Connecticut. Two more foundational documents can be traced to these colonies.

The Fundamental Orders of Connecticut, adopted in 1639, is considered the first American constitution. The Rev. Thomas Hooker's sermon from Deut. 1:13 [the passage quoted earlier about the people of Israel choosing their leaders] formed the cornerstone for this constitution. The document begins by acknowledging that "the word of God requires that to maintain the peace and union of such a people there should be an orderly and decent government established according to God," partly "to maintain and preserve the liberty and purity of the gospel of our Lord Jesus." It then speaks of the colonial legislature and says that if a law is not in effect to cover a situation that may arise, the government should judge "according to the rule of the word of God."[22]

Massachusetts, in 1641, passed the Body of Liberties. This document is the first American bill of rights. A minister, Nathaniel Ward, was the author. Its preamble claims that civil liberties have their basis in Christianity. Ninety-eight "laws" comprise the Body of Liberties, all concerned with the potential tyranny of the government and the rights and privileges of citizens. Some issues addressed are illegal arrests, equality under the law, keeping property secure against government intrusions, freedom of speech and petition, and the right of lawsuit if other rights are abridged.

The Declaration of Independence already has been discussed, but it is worth noting again that the basis of the Declaration was the "unalienable" rights given to men by the Creator. These rights were no longer being protected by government, so it was the duty of citizens to alter or abolish such government and set up a new government that would take its responsibilities seriously.

This brings us to the Constitution. A study of intellectual influences upon Americans at that time reveals a potent fact. As the author of the study states, "If we ask what book was most frequently cited by Americans during the founding era, the answer somewhat surprisingly is: the book of Deuteronomy."[23]

The author goes on to state that this is due to the high number of sermons dealing with civil government. While some scholars may wish to exclude sermons as a source of political thinking, to do so would be to misunderstand the founding era. It was common for ministers to speak on political themes. There was no artificial separation between church and state. Election sermons in New England, given right before general elections, always called the people to a consideration of righteous government and urged them to give their votes to representatives who would carry out God's will on earth.

The same study notes that the second most cited source was writers of the moderate Enlightenment, men such as John Locke and Montesquieu. While some question their Christian faith, there can be little argument as to the Biblical framework of their political thinking. Locke was a revolutionary writer, but only in the sense that he wrote against the divine right of kings in favor of representative government.[24] Montesquieu was widely quoted by the founding fathers because he wrote eloquently of the necessity for balanced government through the separation of powers. In his *The Spirit of Laws* he gives his philosophical presuppositions:

> They who assert that a blind fatality produced the various effects we behold in this world talk very absurdly; for can anything be more unreasonable than to pretend that a blind fatality could be productive of intelligent beings?...

> God is related to the universe, as Creator and Preserver; the laws by which He created all things are those by which He preserves them. He acts according to these rules, because He knows them; He knows them, because He made them; and He made them, because they are in relation to his Wisdom and power.[25]

Montesquieu's presuppositions are consistent with a Christian worldview regardless how he received the whole gospel message.

The American Christian Constitution

The Constitution also is consistent with Biblical principles. The preamble states the reasons for its establishment. First was the desire to form a more perfect union. The Articles of Confederation were destructive of unity and union because the powers were out of balance; the national government was nearly powerless and the states reigned supreme.

The next three reasons were to establish justice, to insure domestic tranquility, and to provide for the common defense. These are all Scriptural. Another reason was to promote the general welfare. The twentieth century reinterpreted this to mean setting up a welfare state. Nothing could have been farther from the minds of those who framed this document. Providing for the general welfare simply meant that the government had the responsibility to make sure that it protected people adequately so that they could prosper in their various callings in life. The government was to maintain a climate of liberty that would benefit everyone. It was not a mandate to create a system that would help specific groups at the expense of everyone else.

The final reason was to secure liberty for the present and future generations. This shows that the founders were not concerned just with their own well-being, but that they wanted to create a government that would stand the test of time and continue to be beneficial to their children and their children's children.

The longest article in the Constitution is the first. It describes the legislative branch and sets up various types of representation, making sure that both individuals and states have a voice in the national government. It also provides, in section eight, a list of the powers of the national government. The list is short. Congress can appropriate money only for the payment of debts, the common defense, and the general welfare (understood in the *general* sense, in which everyone is benefited).

Then the specific ways in which money can be spent are listed. Only sixteen are given; a seventeenth says that any laws necessary and proper for carrying out the first sixteen are acceptable. One searches in vain in this list for anything approaching the welfare system currently in operation. Neither is anything said about education or the arts.

Concerning this list James Madison said, during the debates over ratification of the Constitution, that some people had misconstrued the idea of the government's power. He argued against the Constitution's opponents when they said that section eight "amounts to an unlimited commission to exercise every power which may be alleged to be necessary for the common defense or general welfare." This could lead, he warned, to the idea that the general welfare could be exercised in the destruction of freedom of the press, trial by jury, or whatever else the government decided. That was not the purpose of the framers. He continued:

> But what color can the objection have, when a specification of the objects alluded to by these general terms immediately follows and is not even separated by a longer pause than a semicolon?... For what purpose could the enumeration of particular powers be inserted, if these and all others were meant to be included in the preceding general power? Nothing is more natural nor common than first to use a general phrase, and then to explain and qualify it by a recital of particulars.[26]

Thomas Jefferson, while serving as Secretary of State in 1791, affirmed Madison's view. To consider the Constitution as giving unlimited power to the government to tax and spend on whatever it pleases, Jefferson complained, "would render all the preceding and subsequent enumerations of power completely useless." It would reduce the Constitution to a single phrase, "that of instituting a Congress with power to do whatever would be for the good of the United States; and as they would be the sole judges of the good or evil, it would be also a power to do whatever evil they pleased." He concluded, "Certainly no such universal power was meant to be given them. It was intended to lace them up straitly within the enumerated powers, and those without which, as means, these powers could not be carried into effect."[27]

Jefferson reiterated his position toward the end of his life:

> Our tenet ever was ... that Congress had not unlimited powers to provide for the general welfare, but were restrained to those specifically enumerated; and that, as it was never meant that they should provide for that welfare but by the exercise of the enumerated powers, so it could not have been meant they should raise money for purposes which the enumeration did not place under their action.[28]

Money was to be raised through taxes only for those items enumerated specifically in section eight. This interpretation dominated throughout the first century or more of American constitutional history. President Franklin Pierce, in 1854, vetoed a bill that would have granted government land to states for the benefit of indigent insane persons. Pierce did not oppose helping such persons, but he did oppose this unconstitutional use of tax money.

While it is true that Pierce generally is not considered one of America's best presidents, and his character and administration can be fairly critiqued in numerous ways, he nevertheless understood his constitutional limitations on this particular issue. His argument against the legislation is a classic statement explaining the inappropriateness of government entering the welfare business. "The question presented," Pierce stated, "clearly is upon the constitutionality and propriety of the Federal Government assuming to enter into a novel and vast field of legislation, namely that of providing for the care and support of all those among the people of the United States who by any form of calamity become fit objects of public philanthropy."

Pierce "feelingly" acknowledged the duty of all men to help those who "are subject to want and to disease of body or mind." But he could not find "any authority in the Constitution for making the Federal Government the great almoner of public charity throughout the United States." To do so would "be contrary to the letter and spirit of the Constitution and subversive of the whole theory upon which the Union of these States is founded."[29] Pierce concluded:

> I shall not discuss at length the question of power sometimes claimed for the General Government under the clause of the eighth section of the Constitution, which gives Congress the power "to lay and collect taxes, duties, imposts, and excises, to pay debts and provide for the common defense and general welfare of the United States," because if it has not already been settled upon sound reason and authority it never will be.... It is not a substantive general power to provide for the welfare of the United States, but is a limitation on the grant of power to raise money by taxes, duties, and imposts. If it were otherwise, all the rest of the Constitution, consisting of carefully enumerated and cautiously guarded grants of specific powers, would have been useless, if not delusive.[30]

Both Pierce and Jefferson used the word "useless" to describe the rest of the Constitution if the government had power to legislate on all matters. They were very perceptive. They described the situation in modern America.

Before examining other features of the Constitution, one story is worth telling. Davy Crockett, who is most often associated with frontier legend and the Alamo, served in Congress from 1827-1831, and again from 1833-1835. One day the House of Representatives was ready to vote on a bill to give money to the widow of a naval officer. It was expected to pass without much controversy since it seemed such a humane gesture. But Crockett challenged his colleagues to reject such an unconstitutional appropriation of funds. He declared:

> I have as much respect for the memory of the deceased, and as much sympathy for the sufferings of the living, if suffering there be, as any man in this House, but we must not permit our respect for the dead or our sympathy for a part of the living to lead us into an act of injustice to the balance of the living. I will not go into an argument to prove that Congress has no power to appropriate this money as an act of charity. Every member upon this floor knows it. We have the right, as individuals, to give away as much of our own money as we please in charity; but as members of Congress we have no right so to appropriate a dollar of the public money. Some eloquent appeals have been made to us upon the ground that it is a debt due the deceased. Mr. Speaker, the deceased lived long after the close of the war; he was in office to the day of his death, and I have never heard that the government was in arrears to him.
>
> Every man in this House knows it is not a debt. We cannot, without the grossest corruption, appropriate this money as the payment of a debt. We have not the semblance of authority to appropriate it as charity. Mr. Speaker, I have said we have the right to give as much money of our own as we please. I am the poorest man on this floor. I cannot vote for this bill, but I will give

one week's pay to the object, and if every member of Congress will do the same, it will amount to more than the bill asks.[31]

The bill did not pass.

Article two of the Constitution outlines the duties of the executive branch headed by the president. Article three focuses on the judicial branch and outlines its authority. There never was any doubt that the federal judiciary could declare state laws unconstitutional if they trespassed the authority of the national Constitution. Although there was some controversy over whether the judiciary could declare an act of Congress unconstitutional, Alexander Hamilton had argued in the *Federalist Papers* that "the interpretation of the laws is the proper and peculiar province of the courts." The judges were to regard the Constitution as the fundamental law and judge all acts in light of constitutional provisions. "If there should happen to be an irreconcilable variance between the two," he counseled, "that which has the superior obligation and validity ought, of course, to be preferred; or, in other words, the Constitution ought to be preferred to the statute, the intention of the people to the intention of their agents."[32]

What about the possibility that the courts themselves "may substitute their own pleasure to the constitutional intentions of the legislature"? The role of the courts, says Hamilton, is merely to declare the sense of the law, "and if they should be disposed to exercise WILL instead of JUDGMENT, the consequence would equally be the substitution of their pleasure to that of the legislative body."[33] In Hamilton's view, this would be as wrong as a legislative body ignoring the Constitution.

Hamilton, however, found it difficult to conceive of the courts becoming a problem. He felt that the judiciary would be the least dangerous to political rights of any of the three branches. After all, it could not tax and spend like the legislative; neither could it wield the sword like the executive. "It may truly be said to have neither FORCE nor WILL but merely judgment; and must ultimately depend upon the aid of the executive arm even for the efficacy of its judgments."[34] This was sufficient for Hamilton to declare the judiciary "beyond comparison the weakest of the three departments of power" and "in continual jeopardy of being overpowered, awed, or influenced by its co-ordinate branches."[35] If Hamilton could have been a witness to American government since the 1930s, he undoubtedly would have changed his mind.

Article four treats the state-state and nation-state relationships. Each state must respect the laws of the other states and citizens of one state have the same rights when they enter a different state. The national government also guarantees that every state will maintain a republican form of government. This means it is the responsibility of the national level to make sure that representation remains intact throughout the country. If a state government denied representation and set up a totalitarian system within the state, it would be the duty of the national government to intervene. That is how important the republican system was to the founders.

The amendment procedure is the subject of article five. It recognizes that the judgment of the founders may not have been perfect and keeps the door open for changes. In the spirit of federalism, however, three-fourths of the states must agree to any alteration in the national Constitution.

Some believe the amendment procedure, designed to make changes few in number and not hastily conceived, is too cumbersome. Consequently, political activists have turned to the courts to try to force changes. This is one

reason why the courts have overstepped their boundaries and have taken on legislative functions.

Article six discusses the authority of the national
Constitution. The article declares it to be the supreme
law of the land, and state laws must not contradict it.
Some, though, have taken this declaration too far and
have forgotten (deliberately?) the federal framework
within which the Constitution operates. "It will not, I presume, have escaped observation" warns Hamilton, "that it
expressly confines this supremacy to laws made *pursuant
to the Constitution.*" He continues with an example:

> Though a law, therefore, for laying a tax for the use of
> the United States would be supreme in its nature and
> could not legally be opposed or controlled, yet a law
> for abrogating or preventing the collection of a tax laid
> by the authority of a State ... would not be the supreme
> law of the land, but a usurpation of power not granted
> by the Constitution.[36]

In other words, if the national government should attempt
to enact any law for which it does not have explicit
authority in the Constitution, the national government
would be acting unconstitutionally. The "Supreme Law of
the Land Clause" is not an invitation to absolute power; it
operates within the confines of the federal system.

Some states ratified the Constitution on the condition
that a Bill of Rights would be added to it. Consequently, in
1791, the first ten amendments were ratified and became
known as the American Bill of Rights. These amendments
were in the spirit of federalism because they were guarantees against the power of the national government, to
ensure that the government's power would be limited
and could never cross certain boundaries.

The First Amendment is probably the most famous. It
declares that "Congress shall make no law respecting an

establishment of religion, or prohibiting the free exercise thereof." Notice that this is a specific limitation on the power of *Congress*. There was to be no official national religion (Christianity must be based on voluntary unity and union); neither could the national government inhibit anyone from worshiping God according to the dictates of his conscience. This says nothing about what the states could do; it was directed at the national government only. The rest of the amendment provides for freedom of speech, of the press, for peaceable assembly, and for petition for redress of grievances.

The Second Amendment protects the right to bear arms; the Third forbids the quartering of soldiers in private homes; the Fourth is protection against unreasonable searches and seizures. Several legal guarantees are covered in the Fifth Amendment: the need for a grand jury indictment for a capital crime; protection against being tried more than once for the same offense; safety of life, liberty, and property through due process of law; and no compulsion to be a witness against oneself.

Amendments Six through Eight detail legal rights such as trial by jury and reasonable punishments. The Ninth explains that rights other than the ones listed in the first eight amendments still exist, and the Tenth, the proposed safeguard of the federal system, says that "the powers not delegated to the United States by the Constitution, nor prohibited by it to the States, are reserved to the States respectively, or to the people." The purpose of all these amendments was to provide additional protection against the power of unlimited government.

This short examination of the Constitution has made the following points: there are specifically enumerated powers for which the national government can enact laws; to go beyond those powers would be to act unconstitutionally; the judicial branch is to judge only and not enter into legislative functions; the only legitimate way to increase the powers of the national government is through the amendment process, not the courts. A review of twentieth-century constitutional history will reveal that all these easily understood points have been violated.

The Fate of the Constitution in the Twentieth Century

One cannot put a specific date on the beginning of the all-out assault on the Constitution. The attack on its integrity began in the nineteenth century, but no major damage was done until early in the twentieth. The presidency of Woodrow Wilson opened the doors for more intrusive government, particularly during World War I, but the Republican administrations of the 1920s reverted back to more constitutionally sound positions. The greatest changes came in the 1930s. In the midst of the Great Depression, Franklin D. Roosevelt won the 1932 presidential election. FDR was willing to do almost anything to restore American prosperity, even if it meant ignoring the letter of the Constitution. Shortly after his inauguration, he embarked on a program he called the New Deal, which was a hastily thrown together series of government actions based on a combination of a pragmatic philosophy and a socialist vision of government.

For the first time the national government entered areas where it had no constitutional authority. FDR called in all gold held by private individuals; it now belonged to the government. Citizens were given Federal Reserve Notes instead, and FDR's administration made them "legal tender." That was not constitutional. The Constitution calls for silver and gold coins only to be legal tender in payment of debts. Federal Reserve Notes are not silver or gold; neither is there any silver or gold backing them up.

Government set up insurance for bank deposits, paid subsidies to farmers to take land out of production, operated an electric utility, created thousands of government jobs for the unemployed, instituted wage and price controls, established a minimum wage, built low-income housing, passed laws for rent control, and provided a system of old age, unemployment, and disability insurance through Social Security. All these actions were in direct violation of both the letter and the spirit of the Constitution. FDR and Congress disregarded the enumerated powers of article one, section eight.

Court tests followed. FDR's National Industrial Recovery Act had created the National Recovery Administration (NRA). This act provided for "codes of fair practices" that governed production, prices, and labor relations. In the 1935 *Schechter Poultry Corporation v. U.S.* Supreme Court case, the Court struck down the NRA as unconstitutional because it allowed the president to legislate rather than simply carry out acts of Congress.

Shortly thereafter, in 1936, in *U.S. v. Butler*, the Court struck down the Agricultural Adjustment Act as unconstitutional. This act paid farmers to take land out of production. In its statement of rejection, the Court held fast to constitutional limitations and the integrity of the federal system. "This act invades the reserved rights of the states," explained the Court. "It is a statutory plan to regulate and control agricultural production, a matter beyond the powers delegated to the federal government." The opinion continued:

> From the accepted doctrine that the United States is a government of delegated powers, it follows that those not expressly granted, or reasonably to be implied from such as are conferred, are reserved to the states or to the people. To forestall any suggestion to the contrary, the Tenth Amendment was adopted. The same propo-

sition, otherwise stated, is that powers not granted are prohibited. None to regulate agricultural production is given, and therefore legislation by Congress for that purpose is forbidden.[37]

The Court invoked both the enumerated powers and the Tenth Amendment in its support. It was a constitutionally sound decision.

Yet in two 1937 cases, the Court reversed itself. In *Helvering v. Davis* the Court stood the Constitution on its head when it decided that the Social Security Act was constitutional because the general welfare clause of article one, section eight was a *positive grant of power*, and that it was up to Congress to decide which laws promoted the general welfare. By this decision, the Court concluded that the enumerated powers in section eight were not limitations on Congress, but merely examples of what kinds of legislation could be passed. This interpretation was unprecedented. Congress now could legislate on *all matters whatsoever*, if it chose to do so.

The second case, *National Labor Relations Board v. Jones and Laughlin Steel Corporation*, dismissed all previous rulings on the interstate commerce clause, ruling that congressional authority could extend to *intrastate* commerce if that activity *might* affect, *even indirectly*, interstate commerce. By 1942 this new precedent became laughable in *Wickard v. Filburn*:

> Farmer Filburn raised more grain than the regulations allowed, but fed the excess grain to his pigs. How, he asked, could the grain I raise on my own farm and feed to my own pigs, possibly be considered interstate commerce? The Court answered: If you hadn't raised grain on your own farm and fed it to your pigs, you might have bought some grain on the market and fed it to your pigs; and that might have affected the price

of grain in interstate commerce! Thus the judge's gavel becomes a judicial magic wand, and the distinction between interstate and intrastate, production and commerce, is miraculously swept away. Another constitutional barrier to Big Government fell by the wayside.[38]

The First Amendment's religion clauses became a battleground beginning in 1947 with the *Everson v. Board of Education* case. The first judicial innovation in this case was the decision to use the Fourteenth Amendment as a tool against the states. The Fourteenth Amendment was added to the Constitution in 1868 to guarantee civil rights for ex-slaves.

In *Everson* the Court, using the Fourteenth Amendment's guarantee of civil rights, ruled that the Bill of Rights applied to the states. Again, this set the Constitution on its head. The Bill of Rights was added to the Constitution to *limit* the power of the national government. By one Supreme Court decision, the national government became the overseer of the application of the Bill of Rights to the states, thus increasing the power of the national government significantly. It could now rule on whether states were providing all these guarantees. While this might sound fine on the surface, it made the national government Big Brother over everyone.

The Supreme Court knew it was using the Fourteenth Amendment to overturn limitations on the national government. As Justice William O. Douglas commented on the due process clause of the amendment: "Due Process ... is the wild card that can be put to such use as the judges choose." Constitutional scholar Raoul Berger has noted: "The Fourteenth Amendment is the case study par excellence of what Justice Harlan described as the Supreme Court's 'exercise of the amending power,' its continuing revision of the Constitution under the guise of interpretation."[39] Consequently, the law can be whatever a judge wants it to be; it is totally arbitrary.

Another bad consequence of *Everson* was the argument of Justice Hugo Black when he asserted that a wall of separation existed between church and state, a wall that was "high and impregnable." He went on to declare that government cannot pass laws that "aid one religion, aid all religions, or prefer one religion over another." In effect, he was saying that all religion had to be excised from the government. This created an official national religion, secular humanism, which says that man is everything and God is irrelevant.

Black's wall of separation has become the cornerstone of all Supreme Court decisions on the "Establishment Clause" of the First Amendment. Yet he based his argument on faulty historical information. Black relied on briefs supplied by the American Civil Liberties Union (ACLU), which took an 1802 letter from Thomas Jefferson to some Baptists as the grounds for a sweeping declaration of secularization. Jefferson's "wall of separation" phrase, taken in context, was a promise to the Baptists that the national government would never impinge on their religious liberty. Its intent was protection *for* the church, not protection *from* the church.

The 1954 *Brown v. Board of Education of Topeka* Supreme Court decision established another shaky precedent. The case involved the civil rights of blacks, questioning whether it was proper to have separate-but-equal facilities, or if society should be more integrated. Again, on the surface it seems only fair that all men made in God's image be treated equally and with due respect. The quarrel is not with that proposition; it is with the manner by which the decision was made. The Court based its decision on the testimony of sociologists and psychologists rather than on legal grounds. As one scholar notes, the Court "was substituting social science for the Constitution and laws as the basis of a legal decision. To do that was to cast judicial restraint to the winds and to engage in judicial legislation on a grand scale."[40] The intent was good, but, in the process, the Constitution was ignored again.

A further departure from a constitutional federal republic began in the 1960s. The pattern begun in the New Deal expanded during President Lyndon B. Johnson's attempt to impose his "Great Society" program on America.

LBJ was a master of legislative maneuvering. This ability, plus the memory of the slain President Kennedy, enabled him to push through a major program of supposed civil rights and antipoverty measures. As radical as the New Deal had been, the Great Society went one step further. The New Deal had kept the distinction between the deserving and undeserving poor. Johnson, however, adopted a system of permanent income transfers from one segment of society to another. His administration moved more into the idea that poverty was a problem with the system [i.e., capitalism], not the individual. Consequently, it was the government's responsibility to help all people. Any restraint that might have remained from consideration of constitutional limitations on power disappeared.

Great Society legislation poured forth in 1965-1966. Medicare and Medicaid were attached to Social Security; new government departments (Housing and Urban Development; Transportation) were established; a National Foundation of the Arts and Humanities gave financial assistance to painters, actors, dancers, musicians, professors, and others; and for the first time the national government got deeply involved with education, both in elementary and secondary schools and in colleges and universities.

Wherever the money flowed, regulations tagged along, and the national government began to dictate terms for receiving the money. States, sensing the new vistas opening to them through the federal purse, became mere appendages of the national level, doing whatever they were told to receive the funds. Federalism was still intact on paper, but was for all purposes nearly extinct.

Even the Civil Rights Act of 1964 had unintended results. Some senators and congressmen resisted it for racial reasons, but others were concerned about the constitutional implications. Would this act lead to preferential treatment for minorities? Never, said its supporters. To show they were serious, Title VII of the act stated:

> Nothing contained in this title shall be interpreted to require any employer ... to grant preferential treatment to any individual or to any group because of race, color, religion, sex, or national origin of such individual or group on account of an imbalance which may exist with respect to the total number or percentage of persons of any race ... employed by an employer ... in comparison with the total number or percentage of persons of such race ... in any community, State, section, or other area, or in the available work force in any community, State, section, or other area.[41]

The act intended to promote legal colorblindness, not preferential treatment—legal equality, not legal reverse discrimination.

Although this prohibition was written specifically into the act, the Supreme Court eventually chose to ignore it altogether. In a 1979 case, *United Steelworkers of America v. Weber*, the Court ruled on whether it was constitutional for the company to set aside 50 percent of its positions in a craft worker training program for minorities. Weber, a white worker rejected for the program, had more seniority than some blacks accepted into the program. He argued that this was discrimination based on race. The Court acknowledged that the set-asides went against a literal reading of Title VII, but claimed that to accept a literal reading would go against the spirit and purpose of the entire Civil Rights Act. The justices rejected Weber's argument.

This case is particularly instructive because it shows how far the legal system has departed from its origins. The Court dismissed the actual words of a Congressional act and the intent of those words as irrelevant. They were sacrificed for the Court's own sociological goal.

Perhaps the clearest decision in flouting the intent of the Constitution was the *Roe v. Wade* abortion case in 1973. The Court found a right to abortion that had gone unnoticed for nearly two centuries. It declared a vague "right to privacy," based on the Ninth Amendment's declaration that other rights existed that were not mentioned in the first eight amendments. This right to privacy was not clearly defined and was merely presumed to extend to abortion. Yet government has always set limits on the actions of individuals and families, as witnessed by divorce laws and laws against euthanasia.

The decision further said that the word "person" in the Fourteenth Amendment's protection of the right to life did not apply to the unborn. Justice Harry Blackmun, who wrote the decision, refused to declare when human life begins, but in practice he did exactly that, because hunters do not shoot at an object in the forest if it *may* be a human being. Blackmun was in fact saying that the unborn child is not a human being—go ahead and shoot!

Pro-life forces hoped that the *Planned Parenthood v. Casey* decision in 1992 would finally reverse *Roe v. Wade.* They were disappointed. The Court, while upholding certain state restrictions on abortion, refused to back down on the 1973 ruling, reaffirming the right to an abortion. One of the most interesting comments in the decision was that "there is a limit to the amount of error that can plausibly be imputed to prior courts." In other words, it is not good to admit to past mistakes. It is preferable to continue in those mistakes rather than correct them. "If the Court's legitimacy should be undermined," the majority opinion lectured, "then, so would the country be in its very ability to see itself through its constitutional ideals."[42] Better to maintain *Roe's* "right" to an abortion than to change a Court decision almost twenty years old. A twenty-year-old Court decision took priority over the Constitution itself.

Justice Antonin Scalia, writing in dissent in *Casey,* quoted Abraham Lincoln: "If the policy of this Government upon vital questions affecting the whole people is to be irrevocably fixed by decisions of the Supreme Court,... the people will have ceased to be their own rulers." Scalia also drew a parallel with the awful *Dred Scott* decision in 1857 that declared that blacks were not citizens, and quoted from a dissent in that case:

> When a strict interpretation of the Constitution, according to fixed rules which govern the interpretation of laws, is abandoned, and the theoretical opinions of individuals are allowed to control its meanings, we have no longer a Constitution; we are under the government of men, who for the time being have power to declare what the Constitution is, according to their own views of what it ought to mean.[43]

Roe opened the floodgates. Now America is besieged by homosexual rights, children's rights, animal rights, and the rights of "Mother Earth." Meanwhile, the rights of Christians are attacked. Where is the Constitution in all this? Why have we come to this juncture? Why has American society reaped this whirlwind? Might it have something to do with what we have sown for the past century and a half? That is the subject of the next chapter.

CHAPTER 8

SOWING AND REAPING: THE BITTER HARVEST

The principle of sowing and reaping is a fitting way to end this study. This is the principle that explains exactly what has gone wrong in American society and government. The apostle Paul, in his letter to the Galatians, warns,

> Do not be deceived, God is not mocked; for whatever a man *sows*, this he will also *reap*. For the one who *sows* to his own flesh shall from the flesh *reap* corruption, but the one who *sows* to the Spirit shall from the Spirit *reap* eternal life.[1]

Sowing means to scatter seed in the ground for the purpose of growth. The ground, applied to people, refers to the heart. The parable of the sower is applicable. A man scatters seed on different types of ground. Some falls beside the road and is trampled underfoot and eaten by birds. Other seed falls on rocky soil and then withers away. Some seed falls among the thorns and is choked as it grows. Finally, some seed lands in good ground and produces a substantial crop.

Jesus explains the parable this way: the seed is God's Word; the roadside symbolizes people who hear the Word, but Satan snatches it from them; rocky soil speaks of those who hear the Word with joy, but fail to take root, and fall away; the soil with thorns refers to people who allow the worries of life to choke out the Word; the good ground stands for those who hold fast to the Word and bear fruit.[2]

Reaping means to receive as a reward. That which is reaped can be good or bad, depending on what is sown. In the parable, each type of ground reaped a certain harvest. The key was the ground in which the seed was sown.

This parable assumes good seed. The definition of seed is "that from which anything springs," or "*principles*." Sowing and reaping tells us that the principles we sow in the hearts of individuals will produce a crop. If our principles are godly, the crop will be Biblical; if the principles are humanistic, the crop will be man-centered. There is a direct connection between the type of principles sown and the type of society and government we reap. It is of the utmost importance, therefore, that Christians promote Biblical principles in both society and government.

The primary means for promoting principles is through education. Webster's original definition of education had four components. He declared education to be a series of instruction and discipline intended to:

1) enlighten the understanding;
2) correct the temper;
3) form manners and habits; and
4) fit a person for usefulness.

Probably no one would argue with education being a means for enlightening the understanding. The starting point for all education is greater knowledge and comprehension. Yet head knowledge, by itself, is not true education.

Webster's second component—correcting the temper—is the character element. The "temper," according to Webster, is the disposition of the mind regarding passions and affections. It encompasses the principles of self-government and Christian character, and acknowledges the necessity for correction. All education develops a type of character, whether Biblical or humanistic values clarification. In values clarification, however, each person has his own idea of right and wrong without reference to any eternal standard. Often schools tell parents that they are concentrating on character development; what they don't say is that they are teaching values clarification.

The third aspect of education—forming manners and habits—is the result of character development. If a person's education promotes Biblical character, his way of life—manners and habits—will reflect righteousness. He will be *trained in righteousness*. A values clarification environment will result in moral relativism.

The last part of the definition—fitting a person for usefulness—is the practical application. A person is enlightened in his understanding, receives character instruction, and forms a way of life to be useful. Too often, this component has been reduced to training in manual skills, without enlightened understanding, character development, or formation of manners and habits. A Biblical approach, which sees each individual as made in the image of God, wants all elements of education to come together as one.

Educational principles in early America were Biblical. These principles created a society based on Biblical beliefs and produced a Biblical understanding of government. They also erected a government patterned after God's original plan for Old Testament Israel.

Biblical seeds were sown first by the Pilgrims and Puritans. One Massachusetts education law, the "Old Deluder Satan Law," passed in the 1640s, warned against illiteracy and the use Satan could make of ignorance. Harvard was founded in 1636 to insure that Biblical education would flourish. The settlers dreaded leaving "an illiterate Ministery to the Churches, when our present Ministers shall lie in the Dust." The focus of the college was clear:

> Let every Student be plainly instructed, and earnestly pressed to consider well, the maine end of his life and studies is, to know God and Jesus Christ which is eternall life, John 17:3 and therefore to lay Christ in the bottome, as the only foundation of all sound knowledge and Learning.[3]

Puritan "public" schools operated in much the same way as the churches. They were locally controlled and financed. Local committees whose members belonged to the church set the standards. Often, the town's pastor served as the schoolteacher. There was no artificial separation of religion and education.

In spite of laws promoting public education, private schools dominated. American education, until the Civil War, was largely in the hands of private academies. More than one generation learned to read and spell because of Noah Webster's Speller, not because of a statewide "system." There was great reliance on individual initiative; people were literate because they were self-motivated.

Throughout America there were free schools established without government control. States and individuals would pay the tuition of those who could not afford it. Few children who desired an education were denied. A survey in Boston in 1817 revealed that 96 percent of all children in the city were attending school and the other 4 percent could have attended charity schools if their parents had chosen that option.[4]

State-controlled education never developed a large following in early America. First, there was the fear that a government-operated educational system would force a uniformity of thought that would endanger liberty. Second, many citizens did not like the taxes needed to pay for it. Third, the consensus was that education was not primarily a function of the government, but was the proper domain of the parents, the church, and the locality.

Since parents controlled most of the schooling through churches, Biblical seeds were sown and early generations maintained a Biblical worldview. Government, even beyond the Civil War, remained true both to the spirit and the letter of the Constitution in most instances. Yet other seeds were beginning to sprout.

The New Seeds

America's Christians in the first half of the nineteenth century had a high regard for science. They looked to it as an expression of God's creation and believed that it was a tool for revealing the glory of God. The tendency for some, however, was to consider science almost as an alternative to the gospel. They tied their presentation of the gospel so closely to scientific proofs that the gospel rose or fell with its agreement with science.

Christians too easily equated progress in science as progress in Christian civilization. Most believed in a post-millennial view of the Second Coming, which said that Christ would return after the world improved enough to receive Him. They rejoiced in the new scientific breakthroughs (the railroad, telegraph, sewing machine, etc.), as a sign of the return of the Savior.

Then came Darwin. His evolutionary interpretation provided an alternative to the Christian view. Props were kicked out from under those who had placed so much reliance on science as an aid to salvation. Evolution soon became the cornerstone for all learning; it replaced the Bible as the foundation for education.

Education already had been changing in the two decades before Darwin. Educational reformers had a model—the Prussian system. Prussia was a militaristic nation in what is now part of Germany. Prussian education declared the state to be absolute; individuals were important only in proportion to their service to the state. The system had a uniform curriculum to enforce conformity of thought; the state trained all teachers, to ensure the teaching of state-approved concepts only; compulsory attendance laws were established so that no one would be exempt from the system; and parents were punished if they refused to cooperate.

This Prussian system was totally incompatible with America's Biblical principles. It made the government more important than the individual, destroyed the self-government of families, made children the property of the state, and forced a unity of thought completely inconsistent with the spirit of unity and union. So who were these reformers and why were they so captivated by this system? Three groups pushed for educational reform. The first group was the Unitarians, who denied the deity of Jesus, and believed that man was ultimately perfectible through education. They perceived education as the cure-all for society's ills.

Unitarians were especially prominent in Massachusetts; their influence made it the first to adopt state-controlled education. Horace Mann, first secretary of the Massachusetts state board of education, was a fervent Unitarian, devoted to stripping education of "sectarian" influences. What he meant by sectarian was church-controlled. Although he promoted the use of the Bible in schools, the focus was entirely on morals; teaching theology was discouraged.

A second group pushing for the Prussian system was the followers of Robert Owen, an English socialist/communist who had attempted to set up a utopian communistic society in New Harmony, Indiana. That experiment failed because, according to Owen, Americans were too wedded to concepts of individuality and private property. He liked the Prussian system because he envisioned it educating Americans out of such ideas.

One of Owen's primary vehicles for promulgating his views was the Working Men's Party. This political party was pro-socialist, anti-Christian, and pro-public education. Orestes A. Brownson, who later converted to Christianity, was an integral part of this party before his conversion. He later wrote about its aims:

> The purpose in the formation of this party was to get control of the political power of the state, so as to be able to use it for establishing our system of schools. We hoped, by linking our cause with the ultra-democratic sentiment of the country, which had ... an anti-Christian character, by professing ourselves the bold and uncompromising champions of equality, by expressing a great love for the people, and a deep sympathy with the laborer, whom we represented as defrauded and oppressed by his employer, by denouncing all proprietors as aristocrats, and by keeping the more unpopular features of our plan as far in the background as possible, to enlist the majority of the American people under the banner of the Working-Men's Party; nothing doubting that, if we could once raise the party to power, we could use it to secure the adoption of our educational system.[5]

Although the Unitarians did not accept the socialist vision of the Owenites, from their different perspectives each worked to undermine the private education of the day. They probably would not have succeeded, due to their relatively small numbers, if it had not been for another ally—the evangelical Protestants.

A growing number of evangelicals in the 1830s and 1840s looked with favor on the Prussian system, but for a different reason. Those decades saw a change in the religious balance in America. More Catholics than before were entering the country and becoming voting citizens. This frightened the Protestant majority, who still feared that Catholics would have a greater allegiance to the pope than to the government. What could be done to protect the Protestant character of America? Many Protestant educators saw a solution in the coercive Prussian system: force Catholic children to attend public schools where they would be trained in the Protestant faith, thereby countering the influence of their parents and priests. Ironically, the Protestants never achieved their goal. Catholic churches started their own schools and foiled the attempt to coerce their children into Protestantism.

The added weight of evangelical Protestants gave the public school forces greater impetus. By the middle of the nineteenth century, public education became dominant. By allying with the Unitarians and Owenites, and by supporting a coercive education system, the Protestants violated the Biblical principles that had made America solidly Christian in the first place.

The Influence of Evolution

Evolutionary theory combined with coercive education policies to alter the nature of American education. Evolutionary ideas affected every academic field, and the practice of education itself soon reflected the new evolutionary thrust.

A certain logic flows from evolutionary views. If evolution is defined as the belief that the universe is the product of the combination of time, chance, and matter, and that all things develop from simple to complex, the door is opened first to the idea that there may be no transcendent god who created all things.

Of course, some people are theistic evolutionists and believe that God is in charge of evolution, but one searches in vain for any Biblical backing for this view. The book of Genesis has to undergo more than a mere reinterpretation to promote it. Most theistic evolutionists, however, do not worry about making the Bible support evolution; they have discarded any attempt to reconcile the two and have opted to embrace evolution's explanation instead.

For most early proponents of evolution, the greatest premise in the theory was that God was unnecessary. Natural processes could account for all life. Given enough time, and the existence of matter (and it would be impolite to ask where matter came from), they could believe that chance developments led to the complexity of the modern world.

Why would someone want to believe this? If there were no god, then man was not created by a god and is not accountable to any higher power. There would be no sin; problems would be merely the result of the lack of evolutionary progress. Allow more time to pass and man will be perfected eventually. If there is no sin, there is no atonement for sin, no supernatural, heaven, or hell. Man can live for himself—a rebel's dream come true.

A second result of evolutionary logic is the depersonalization of man. Since he is not created in the image of a god, and there is no divine purpose in his being, he is simply a cosmic accident, a chance development of matter.

He is nothing more than a mass of chemicals. If that is all there is to man, then he is not intrinsically valuable. That blob of tissue developing inside a pregnant woman is simply that—a blob of tissue. If the woman feels it is too inconvenient to have a child, there is no guilt in ridding herself of it. After all, it is not human yet. Euthanasia is the other end of the spectrum, and we are beginning to see that come to the surface now. Evolutionary logic encourages both abortion and euthanasia.

A third result of evolutionary logic is that there are no absolute moral standards. If there is no god and if man is a mass of chemicals, where is the source of morality? How can we know what is right and wrong? Are the concepts of right and wrong "wrong" in themselves? If so, who is to judge? In practical terms, each person is to decide for himself what he considers to be right and wrong, without reference to any eternal requirements. He then adapts his personal moral beliefs to society's, so that he will fit in with the "norm." This makes society the ultimate judge of right and wrong, and those judgments could change with each new intellectual fad.

This is moral relativism, which says that truth is dependent upon time, place, and individual experience. What may have been "right" for the Hebrews in an earlier era, may be outdated and unworkable today. Moral relativists abhor the idea that an old system of theology or morality should dominate a more "enlightened" people. Moral relativism, based on evolutionary theory that denies a meaningful god, and which makes man a cosmic accident, now permeates society and every field of academic study.

One of the first fields affected was sociology. An English sociologist, Herbert Spencer, took Darwin's theory and applied it to society. His followers called it Social Darwinism. Spencer believed that societies progressed automatically from one evolutionary phase to another. He excluded a personal god and only noted that a force was somehow making this happen, a force he called "The Unknowable." Evolutionary progress would ultimately lead to a perfectly adapted, perfectly harmonious society, inhabited by perfect people. The key question is, "Adapted to what?" Certainly the Christian worldview would not be included. People who hold unswervingly to Biblical concepts of sin, repentance, and judgment would not "fit" into any society envisioned by Spencer.

Spencer's main American disciple was William Graham Sumner, a Yale sociologist, who commented,

> The great stream of time and earthly things will sweep on just the same in spite of us. It bears with it now all the errors and follies of the past, the wreckage of all the philosophies, the fragments of all the civilizations, the wisdom of all the abandoned ethical systems, the debris of all the institutions, and the penalties of all the mistakes. It is only in imagination that we stand by and look at and criticize it and plan to change it. Every one of us is a child of his age and cannot get out of it. He is in the stream and is swept along with it.[6]

Sumner's evaluation of the sweep of evolutionary history is fatalistic. No one can change anything; it is an illusion to think otherwise. Glorious evolution will transform all in its wake.

Another sociologist, Lester Frank Ward, rejected Spencer and Sumner's notion of how evolution affects society. Ward did not reject evolution, only their interpretation of its application to society. Ward pushed the view that evolution now has advanced far enough that man can contribute to its future course. Man's thinking has developed to the point where he can now direct evolution for his own good. Ward's emphasis was on the good of society, rather than the individual. He believed in a sociocracy, the planned control of society by society. But who speaks for society? Who determines the direction society should go? Who will enforce it? Ward believed the government should enforce it through regulation. Further, he advocated government control of education to direct society in the way it should go.

Lester Frank Ward's approach fit perfectly with the Prussian model of education that first excited the Unitarians and Owenites. It also meshed well with Karl Marx's doctrine of socialism/communism. Marx, in his 1848 *Communist Manifesto*, had promoted extensive government control and regulation, with a government-controlled public education system to create his type of society. This shows the definite link, in this instance, between evolutionary theory and socialist thought.

The strong government championed by Marx and Ward found an ally in the philosophical school of pragmatism. Pragmatism is really just a little different way of looking at relativism. It regards the practical consequences and useful results of ideas as the test of their truthfulness, and considers truth a process, constantly changing with each generation and type of culture. In other words, if it works, it is true. What works for one person in the realm of morals, may not work for another, but whatever works for each person is true for that person. Again, there are no absolutes.

Evolutionary pragmatic philosophy has affected law and government profoundly. Pragmatism changed the concept of law from its eternal basis to a transitory, process-oriented, ever-changing basis. Law no longer starts with the commands of God, but with the needs of men. This is called *sociological* law, revealing again the links among the various strands of thought.

If there are no eternal truths and no absolutes, it is necessary for government to step in and decide right and wrong, thus fitting in nicely with Ward's vision of social engineering.

Christopher Langdell, who began his tenure as Dean of the Harvard Law School in the 1870s, introduced the case law method of teaching. He based this method on the evolutionary, pragmatic belief that law was an evolving process, constantly rewritten in the opinions of the judges. In case law, one looks at previous judicial decisions and uses them as a precedent for deciding a current case. The use of precedent was not new; what was new was the divorce from eternal truths and the emphasis on using more recent precedents. Devotion to the latest decisions, no matter how far removed from the original understanding of a law or the Constitution, became the rule.

The impact was to make the Constitution a "living document," according to sociological law advocates. The Constitution, they say, should be looked upon as an "evolving instrument," to be redefined according to the need of the moment. Why be bound by a previous generation that did not anticipate the needs of the future? Through the case law method, new generations of judges were taught to stretch the Constitution whenever necessary, to the point that whatever the judge says is law, not what the letter of the Constitution may say. It would be wrong, they complain, to hold to the letter when the spirit calls for a change.

They seem to overlook the fact that the Constitution allows for change through amendments. If enough states in this federal republic want a specific change, an amendment can be passed to make it legal. Sociological law, on the other hand, is an *illegal* and *unconstitutional* use of the court system.

Oliver Wendell Holmes, Jr., who served as a Supreme Court justice from 1902-1932, was an early supporter of sociological law and the pragmatic philosophy. He declared that in the development of a body of law "the ultimate question is what do the dominant forces of the community want and do they want it hard enough to disregard whatever inhibitions may stand in the way."[7] This is nothing less than the rule of men rather than the rule of law. Holmes's view denies inalienable rights from the Creator and makes all rights manmade through civil government. It is a repudiation of the Declaration of Independence.

What was Holmes's worldview? Where is God? Who is man? He answers those questions quite eloquently:

> I see no reason for attributing to man a significance different in kind from that which belongs to a baboon or a grain of sand. I believe that our personality is a cosmic ganglion, just as when certain rays meet and cross there is a white light at the meeting point, but the rays go on after the meeting as they did before, so, when certain other streams of energy cross at the meeting point, the cosmic ganglion can frame a syllogism or wag its tail.[8]

For Holmes, man is a chance happening, the result of streams of energy crossing at random. This makes man no better than a baboon or a grain of sand, another example of the depersonalization of man in evolutionary theory.

The previous chapter detailed the manner in which the Constitution was ignored in the twentieth century, from the New Deal to the Great Society. The underlying factors in this dismissal of the Constitution are the acceptance of evolutionary theory as applied to law, the acceptance of Ward's social engineering, and the pragmatic philosophy.

Another key area heavily influenced by evolution and pragmatism is psychology. When Webster defined psychology in 1828, he called it a discourse or treatise on the human soul, or a study of the nature and properties of the soul. He defined soul as the spiritual, rational, and immortal part of man that distinguishes him from the animals. A newer edition of Webster's dictionary, in its description of psychology, leaves out the word soul entirely, focusing instead on the mind and on external behavior. The modern definition of soul says nothing about distinguishing man from the animals. What a difference a new worldview can make!

One of the first applications of evolution to psychological thought was the belief that man is just a higher form of animal. Since animal behavior was the product of responses to environmental stimuli, man's behavior, they asserted, could be studied in the same way. This type of psychology, called behaviorism, saw man as simply another life form to be placed in experiments. Behaviorism believes that man can be conditioned to respond in certain ways, given the right stimuli. In other words, man does not possess a free will, but becomes whatever his environment dictates. He is a human insect whose brief existence is determined by society or nature.

Psychologist B.F. Skinner, one of the most celebrated behaviorists, argued in one of his books, *Beyond Freedom and Dignity*, that man had to divest himself of the belief that he had either freedom or dignity. In this book, Skinner reduced man to little more than a biological organism, whose life is determined by forces out of his control. This is similar to Spencer and Sumner's Social Darwinism. Surely the link to evolutionary theory is obvious in this approach to psychology.

Sigmund Freud, whose psychological school bears his name, was a Jew who hated everything about his

Jewishness. The Old Testament was anathema to him, and he dismissed the idea of a god to whom he was accountable. Evolutionary theory made sense to Freud; he based psychoanalysis on the "truth" of evolution. Psychoanalysis has become mainstream, and Freudian thought has governed the fields of childrearing and criminal justice.[9]

Rogerian psychology, named after Carl Rogers, dominates today. Rogers was an evolutionist also, but endorsed a pantheistic evolution tied to Eastern mysticism. His psychology promotes the cult of the self: each person must concentrate on achieving his full potential and develop himself according to what he wants out of life. The encounter group movement originated in Rogerian psychology. Terminology such as self-image, self-esteem, and self-actualization (with help from psychologist Abraham Maslow) forms the substance of the Rogerian system.

All the answers to one's problems are to be found within oneself; no one can tell you what is right and wrong for you. Neither is anyone supposed to because Rogerian psychology prides itself on being nonjudgmental. This is moral relativism in full bloom. It was Rogerian psychology that gave birth to values clarification in the schools.

Most psychology has redefined sin. The Bible calls drunkenness a sin for which man is accountable; psychology calls it alcoholism, which is genetic in nature and for which man is not accountable. It is a disease, not a sin, in modern psychology. What began with alcoholism has now spread to almost every human behavior. Homosexuality is not a sin, but an orientation to be celebrated; some people are just born that way. Overeating is a disorder, not gluttony. There is a support group for every "disorder" known to man, eager to alter external behavior, while rejecting the root of the problem—sin.

Such groups operate on the belief that people have no choice but to be this way the rest of their lives. Once an alcoholic, always an alcoholic. Yet this flies in the face of Scripture. The apostle Paul tells the Corinthians,

> Do not be deceived; neither fornicators, nor idolaters, nor adulterers, nor effeminate, nor *homosexuals*, nor thieves, nor the covetous, nor *drunkards*, nor revilers, nor swindlers, shall inherit the kingdom of God. And such *WERE* [emphasis mine] some of you; but you were washed, but you were sanctified, but you were justified in the name of the Lord Jesus Christ, and in the Spirit of our God.[10]

Paul, in this passage, calls drunkenness and homosexuality sins, not a genetic disorder or an orientation to be celebrated, respectively. Men are accountable to God for such behavior. Those who practice these sins will not inherit the kingdom of God. Then to underscore the fact that these are not lifelong genetic issues, Paul continues by claiming that the Christians to whom he is writing *used to be* such sinners, but they *are no longer*. That is unacceptable theology to Alcoholics Anonymous, but to whom should Christians look for the truth?

Even reality therapy, which counsels people to acknowledge sin and repent, does so in the context of moral relativism. Do you believe you have committed a sin? Well, if it is a sin to you, get rid of it because that is the only way you will ever get relief from the guilt you are feeling. But you determine whether something is a sin; there is no eternal standard by which you should judge your actions. This is pure pragmatism; it does not lead people to the truth.

One Christian psychology professor has strong words for Christians who wish to mix man's psychology with God's truth:

True Christianity does not mix well with psychology. When you try to mix them, you often end up with a watered-down Christianity instead of a Christianized psychology. But the process is subtle and rarely noticed. I wasn't aware that I was confusing two different things. And others in the church who might have been expected to put me right were under the same enchantment as I. It was not a frontal attack on Christianity—I'm sure I would have resisted that. It was not a case of a wolf at the door: the wolf was already in the fold, dressed in sheep's clothing. And from the way it was petted and fed by some of the shepherds, one would think it was the prize sheep.[11]

The same author also says,

When people hear I'm involved with both psychology and Christianity, they generally assume I'm working on a synthesis to bring the two closer together, to patch up whatever few remaining differences there might be. "Aren't psychology and religion just two different ways of getting at the same thing?"—it's a question I often hear.

It is true that popular psychology shares much in common with Eastern religion; in fact, a merger is well under way. But if you're talking about Christianity, it is much truer to say that psychology and religion are competing faiths. *If you seriously hold to one set of values, you will logically have to reject the other.*[12]

Modern psychology, then, in most of its manifestations, is built on evolutionary behaviorism and pragmatism. It divorces itself from the Christian message of sin, repentance, and faith in the only Son of God. The saddest spectacle of all is when Christians replace clear Biblical counseling with these psychological theories. The authors of one book on a Biblical worldview are right when they say,

> Many Christians we know believe that people's political opinions and actions are determined by economic class, not by theological beliefs. These Christians believe in economic determinism; they would deny being Marxists, but they ... have accepted Marxist dogma. Many Christians believe that we behave as we do because of prior conditioning. They might deny being behaviorists, but they've accepted behaviorist dogma. Many Christians believe that a person's position on moral issues should change as social conditions change. They would deny being relativists, but they've adopted the basic tenets of relativism.[13]

The biological sciences, sociology, political science, and psychology are not the only academic fields affected by evolution. I teach history, and evolutionary thought is evident there also. Most world civilization books begin with a chapter on prehistoric man and how he evolved. These books assume the truth of evolutionary premises concerning the growth of cultures and civilizations. Borrowing from evolutionary anthropology, historians accept the idea that all societies evolve from simple to complex. Further, they teach without hesitation that religious ideas developed similarly. From a simplistic polytheism, man gradually turned to a more sophisticated monotheism. Yet the Bible teaches the opposite. All men knew of the one high God and then civilizations degenerated into idolatrous polytheism. It is time for those who call themselves Christians to make a choice. Which source do they truly believe? If they take their stand with the Word of God, it will affect the way they teach.

Education: The Ground in Which the Seed is Sown

Educational theory and practice also have repudiated the Biblical worldview. Unitarians and Owenites planted the seeds, and evangelical Protestants adopted them for their own particular purpose, but the real destruction of the Biblical worldview in education began after the Civil War.

The public education system, encouraged by the champions of the Prussian structure, grew at an astounding rate. State after state followed the Massachusetts pattern. The National Education Association (NEA), founded in 1857, sought to organize teachers and set standards for the profession. As laudable as the intent may have been, it furthered the idea of centralized education supported by the government. The push for greater professionalization created education "experts" who felt they could decide what was best for American education.

The age of the expert dawned in America in the late nineteenth century, not only in education, but in all professions. The experts, imbued with evolutionary enthusiasm and confident that there could be a scientific approach to all areas of life, tried to make Ward's vision of social engineering a reality. The key was education. Professional educators were convinced there was a science of education. They called themselves "progressive" educators, dedicated to altering both content and methodology.

Edward L. Thorndike of Columbia Teachers College was one of the first educators to wed psychology and education theory. He used evolution as the basis for his belief that students should learn by conditioning, and introduced stimulus-response techniques; true-false and multiple-choice exams replaced essays. Thorndike's philosophy was behaviorist psychology transferred to the classroom. A child was no longer a being made in the image of God, but a higher form of animal. Logical thinking and the organization of thought in essays became secondary considerations; stimulus-response was the new method of learning.

The most influential of all the new professional educators was John Dewey. He was the "Father of Progressive Education." Dewey was an atheist and a socialist, and he sought to imbue American education with those ideals. He was a leader in the American Humanist Association and a signer of the Humanist Manifesto, published in 1933. A brief examination of the Manifesto reveals Dewey's most cherished beliefs.

The Manifesto's first resolution states: "Religious humanists regard the universe as self-existing and not created." Notice they call themselves "religious" humanists. Secular humanism, even by admission of the humanists themselves, is a religion, a worldview, a competitor to the Biblical worldview. They found it essential to begin the Manifesto with an explicit rejection of creation and an affirmation of evolution. This is the starting point for John Dewey.

The second resolution expands on the evolutionary basis by saying, "Humanism believes that man is a part of nature and that he has emerged as the result of a continuous process." The fourth takes evolutionary theory and applies it to society as a whole:

> Humanism recognizes that man's religious culture and civilization, as clearly depicted by anthropology and history, are the product of a gradual development due to his interaction with his natural environment and with his social heritage. The individual born into a particular culture is largely molded to that culture.

The fifth and sixth resolutions aim squarely at belief in God, moral absolutes, and the supernatural: "Humanism asserts that the nature of the universe depicted by modern science makes unacceptable any supernatural or cosmic guarantees of human values.... We are convinced that the time has passed for theism."

The socialist agenda is described in resolution fourteen:

> The humanists are firmly convinced that existing acquisitive and profit-motivated society has shown itself to be inadequate and that a radical change in methods, controls, and motives must be instituted. A socialized and cooperative economic order must be established to the end that the equitable distribution of the means of life be possible. The goal of humanism is a free and universal society in which people voluntarily and intelligently cooperate for the common good. Humanists demand a shared life in a shared world.[14]

John Dewey, then, the "Father of Progressive Education," was a firmly committed "modern man," lacking a belief in God, moral absolutes, the supernatural, private property, and the Biblically based federal republic form of government. These attitudes are evident in his educational approach.

Dewey defined education as that "reconstruction or reorganization of experience which adds to the meaning of experience, and which increases ability to direct the course of subsequent experience."[15] Dewey's experience orientation was the outgrowth of his dismissal of eternal truths. By fostering the idea that all education should rest on experience, he minimized the significance of book learning. The school, Dewey felt, should be an embryonic community, with occupations that reflected the society. Students should help run the school and learn from the experience.

There is usually a grain of truth in error, which is why certain errors are so deceptive. Experience is part of education, but Dewey sought to give it the central place. He stated,

> I believe that the social life of the child is the basis of concentration, or correlation, in all his training or growth.... I believe, therefore, that the true center of correlation on the school subjects is not science, nor literature, nor history, nor geography, but the child's social activities.... I believe, therefore, in the so-called expressive or constructive activities as the center of correlation. I believe that this gives the standard for the place of cooking, sewing, manual training, etc., in the school.[16]

Why this emphasis? What was Dewey's goal? He leaves no doubt:

> The introduction of active occupations, of nature-study, of elementary science, of art, of history; the relegation of the merely symbolic and formal to a secondary position; the change in the moral school atmosphere ... are not mere accidents, they are the necessities of the larger social evolution. It remains but to organize all these factors, to appreciate them in their fulness of meaning, and to put the ideas and ideals involved into complete, uncompromising possession of our school system.[17]

Dewey saw the school as the fertile soil for planting seeds conducive to his atheistic, socialistic enterprise. The changes he introduced were not accidents, but deliberate. As one study of Dewey's educational policies summarizes: "The school's ultimate social ideal was the transformation of society through a new, socially minded individualism."[18] Another notes, "He hoped that through compulsory public education his belief system would ultimately become the sole 'religious faith,' 'the common faith of mankind' that would 'realize the [S]tate as one Commonwealth of truth.'"[19]

The Bitter Harvest

How successful have Dewey and his disciples been? To answer that question, it is necessary to see whether the humanist agenda dominates modern American education. A brief examination of the textbooks currently in use and of the resolutions of the NEA, the nation's largest teachers' union, should provide the answers.

Rather than examine all textbooks in all subjects, since my focus is government, social studies texts should be adequate for a judgment. The first point is that there exists a subject called "social studies." Prior to the ascendancy of Progressive Education, there was no such subject. Children learned history, geography, and government, but not social studies. The name originates in the socialist worldview; it lumps together history, government, and geography into a mishmash that emphasizes society and socialization.

Paul Vitz, an educational psychologist, already has done original research in this area. Ironically, the study was funded by a government agency, the National Institute of Education, part of the Department of Education. It was completed in 1985 during Ronald Reagan's presidency, but not much has changed since then.

The purpose of the study was to find out if public school textbooks were biased or censored. Vitz concluded, "The answer to both is yes. And the nature of the bias is clear: Religion, traditional family values, and conservative political and economic positions have been reliably excluded from children's textbooks."[20] Vitz then documents his conclusion with an amazing array of statistics.

In a study of forty social studies texts for grades 1-4, Vitz found that although the books did talk about some aspects of religion in early America, it was usually treated as old-fashioned and unimportant to modern life. There was almost a total blackout on Christianity in America beyond the colonial period. He found it disturbing "that not one of the forty books totaling ten thousand pages had one *text* reference to a primary religious activity occurring in representative contemporary American life."[21] In fact,

> Today's powerful Protestant religious world of the Bible Belt, of the born-again Christians, of the fundamentalists and of the evangelicals, of the Moral Majority, of Billy Graham, Oral Roberts, Jerry Falwell, the TV evangelists ... this very American Protestant world representing millions of Americans—is without *one* reference in word or image in this sample of forty books.[22]

A significant instance of bias against religion was a text that had thirty pages on the Pilgrims, but not one word that even mentioned their religion. Vitz relates,

> One mother whose son is in a class using this book wrote me to say that he came home and told her that "Thanksgiving was when the Pilgrims gave thanks to the Indians." The mother called the principal ... to point out that Thanksgiving was when the Pilgrims thanked God. The principal responded by saying, "that was her opinion"—the schools could only teach what was in the books![23]

Vitz also examined the approach to the family and to government in these books. He discovered that the definition of family was broad, in one case described simply as "a group of people." Not one text called marriage the foundation of the family and not one featured a woman as a homemaker. On the political front, Vitz concluded,

> Political bias also shows in the reliable tendency of these books to characterize recent (and much of past) American history in terms of three issues or themes: minority rights, feminism, and ecological and environmental issues. In every case, the *pro* position is presented as positive; the opposition is never given any serious treatment. There are no conservative positions identified or supported in any way in any of these books. For example, there is simply no mention of the anti-ERA movement, the pro-life movement, or opposition to affirmative action, or the tax revolt. The idea that government might be too big, too controlling, is never mentioned.[24]

The situation did not improve when Vitz turned to fifth- and sixth-grade texts. *Not one* of the fifth-grade books on American history mentioned the Great Awakening of the eighteenth century, the great revivals of the nineteenth century, or the Holiness and Pentecostal movements. Treatments of the twentieth century showed profound neglect of anything religious.

The sixth-grade world civilization texts were even worse, if that is possible. Mohammed's life got considerably more coverage than the life of Jesus. Two texts talked about Mohammed, but never mentioned Jesus at all. In another, "The rise of Islam, Islamic culture, and Mohammed himself get an eleven-page section, plus other scattered coverage. The rise of Christianity gets almost nothing (a few lines on p. 116). In these books, then, it is not that great religious figures are totally avoided—it is that Jesus is avoided."[25] The Reformation suffers from the same neglect:

> One of the most obvious characteristics of many of the texts is their failure to mention the Protestant Reformation, or their tendency to give it very little emphasis. For example, American Book hardly refers to Protestantism and not at all to the Reformation; Riverside has twenty pages on Tanzania, nineteen pages on the history of the Netherlands, and sixteen pages on ancient Crete, but it makes no reference to Martin Luther or Calvin, and there is almost nothing on Protestantism.... (One commentator on this study noted that a historical treatment "of the Netherlands with no reference to John Calvin or the Reformation ... is roughly equivalent to summarizing the history of the United States without mentioning George Washington or the American Revolution.")[26]

It is not necessary to give examples of what Vitz discovered in high school texts—they were identical to the elementary texts. In all cases the Christian worldview was either missing or sadly neglected, and the type of family life, morals, and government encouraged by Biblical principles was denigrated. Why is this so? The education professionals have sown different seeds, resulting in a different harvest.

What seeds are currently being sown? All that is necessary is to read the resolutions that are passed each year by the National Education Association.[27]

First, it must be understood that the NEA seeks to be the sole voice for American education. It wants to dictate standards for every school. Although it declares that individuals should be "free to choose" private education, all schools "must be accredited under uniform standards established by the appropriate [government] agency in collaboration with the Association [NEA] and its affiliates." This means loss of control by the private schools of what they wish to teach and how they wish to teach it. They would remain private schools in name, but be subject to the NEA/government bureaucracy.

The same rule applies to home schoolers. The NEA goes on record as believing that "home schooling programs cannot provide the student with a comprehensive education experience." Parents who home school must be limited to teaching their own children and all home schoolers "must meet all state requirements" and instruction "should be by persons who are licensed by the appropriate state education licensure agency, and a curriculum approved by the state department of education should be used." If these resolutions were to become law, home schools would be no different from the public schools. But, of course, that is the NEA's goal.

The NEA endorsed Jimmy Carter's presidential campaign in 1976, and the candidacy of every Democratic presidential nominee ever since. When Carter won the 1976 election, he paid back the NEA with a new bureaucracy, the Department of Education. The NEA's resolutions insist that the Department "must be a viable force for the maintenance and improvement of public education in the United States." As evidence that the NEA sees the Department as its own agency, the resolution continues, "The Association ... believes that Association members must be fully involved in establishing goals and planning programs with the Department."

In response to calls for the Department's abolition, the NEA declares, "The Association further believes that internal and external attempts to dismantle and to erode the effectiveness of the Department ... through the federal budgetary process are detrimental to the public interest."

Detrimental to the public interest, or detrimental to the interest of the NEA? The two are not identical.

The NEA opposes any attempt to provide parents with greater educational choice. Parental option plans, according to the NEA, "compromise the Association's commitment to free, equitable, universal, and quality public education for every student." The question begs to be asked: do we currently have free (what are taxes for?), equitable, and quality public education? Wouldn't quality improve with equitable competition from private schools? Currently, there is no equity for parents who put their children in private schools; they have to pay for two systems instead of just one.

Yet the NEA always opposes any attempt to relieve private school parents of the burden of paying for two systems. Tuition tax credits, says the NEA, could "undermine public education, reduce the support needed to adequately fund public education, and have the potential for racial, economic, and social segregation of children." The same scare tactic (and identical wording) is used to oppose voucher plans.

The NEA also denounces sexism and sexual orientation discrimination. It believes that many instructional materials portray females and males in sex-stereotyped roles and wants to "eliminate discrimination and stereotyping in the curriculum, textbooks, resource and instructional materials, activities, etc." The resolution continues: "The Association encourages its affiliates to develop and implement training programs on these matters." Already this is happening in the "Political Correctness" movement, particularly on college campuses. Offenders are forced to take sensitivity training to rid themselves of their sexist heresies. Of course, from a Biblical position, all people are to be treated with respect, but that is not what the NEA means. This is part of the attempt to change the God-given roles of men and women, and fits in nicely with what Vitz discovered in the textbooks—the absence of women from traditional homemaking duties.

Further evidence of the NEA's promotion of the homo-sexual agenda can be found in the resolution on student sexual orientation, which states: "The ... Association believes that all persons, regardless of sexual orientation, should be afforded equal opportunity within the public education system. The Association further believes that, for students who are struggling with their sexual/gender orientation, every school district and educational insti-tution should provide counseling services ... by trained personnel." Who will provide this counseling—pastors of churches who hold to the view that homosexuality is a sin? Hardly. "Trained personnel" will be psychologists or school counselors indoctrinated into humanistic psycho-logical theories. This will be Rogerian "nonjudgmental" counseling that accepts homosexuality as an alternative lifestyle.

The resolution on sex education speaks of community settings and values and respect for individual differences, yet it is also anti-Biblical in its approach. It endorses sex education classes without threat from censorship or law-suits. What this means is that parents cannot object to the content of the classes or try to change the approach. Parents need "orientation" to be sure they see the light. The classes should include teaching on birth control methods (including abortion) and diversity of sexual ori-entation. The latter is an apologetic for the homosexual lifestyle. Perhaps this is the true meaning of the afore-mentioned respect for individual differences. It ends with the statement that knowledge of sexual matters is a "right." Has anyone checked the Constitution lately?

The family planning resolution states unequivocally the "right" to reproductive freedom. Some say this is not an endorsement for abortion, yet this is the identical language used by Planned Parenthood, the National Organization for Women, and the National Abortion Rights Action League to promote abortion on demand. The NEA then goes on to promote the "implementation of community-operated, school-based family planning clinics that will provide intensive counseling by trained personnel." Those trained personnel are almost solidly pro-abortion, and the main activities of these clinics wherever they are set up are to hand out contraceptives and serve as a referral agency for abortion clinics.

What about those who have beliefs contrary to the NEA's? That issue is addressed in a resolution on academic and professional freedom.

> The Association further believes that legislation and regulations that mandate *or permit* [emphasis mine] the teaching of religious doctrines and/or groups that promote anti-public-education agendas violate both student and teacher rights.

The NEA will not *allow* contrary views, even if they are *not mandated*. One of the most visible areas of conflict has been the attempt to allow the teaching of scientific creationism in public education. The NEA will not permit this and fights the effort with all the funding at its disposal. Note also that no one who believes in non-public education can be heard. Everyone must conform to the NEA's version of truth.

The NEA does not limit itself to educational issues. Anything that can in any way be linked to education, or that can be taught in the classroom, is subject to its attention. For instance, the Association takes a stand on National Health Insurance, calling on the government to fund an insurance plan for every American. It also calls access to comprehensive health care a "right" for every resident of the United States, not just citizens. Government funding of health insurance is part of the socialist agenda. A "right" to health care is not found in the Constitution, neither for citizens nor residents, but that does not stop the NEA from advocating that the government [i.e., taxpayers] pay for it.

The NEA also gets into the political arena through resolutions supporting statehood for the District of Columbia, affirmative action programs, the national welfare state, an Equal Rights Amendment for women, environmentalism, and gun control. The NEA is a firm supporter of the United Nations and believes that "peace is superior to war." How much education does one need to believe that? Does it require a doctorate to believe that peace is a preferable state of affairs? The NEA promotes one-world government and urges the United States to participate in the World Court. The danger is whether such participation will damage this country's God-given right to self-government. But the NEA does not mention that concern.

Disarmament is also high on the NEA's agenda, coupled with an overly optimistic view that peace education will take care of conflicts among nations. Defense against external enemies is one of the few specific Biblical purposes of civil government. Shouldn't unbiblical and unconstitutional expenditures be eliminated instead?

These resolutions are only samples of the stances the NEA is taking today. They are almost uniformly humanistic and socialistic. An examination of resolutions not mentioned here would only confirm the statements already made.

The harvest is bitter indeed. The seeds of individuality, self-government, property, unity and union, Christian character, and a Christian form of government are being planted only in individual families and some Christian schools. Since the public education system sows seeds of humanism and socialism almost exclusively, American society and government no longer rest upon those Biblical principles, but on anti-Biblical concepts. Is there any hope for restoration?

CONCLUSION

WHAT CAN THE RIGHTEOUS DO?

———

This book is not meant to be a source of despair. I have tried to balance the Biblical perspective with the current dismal situation. There is a Biblical approach to civil government, and we should be encouraged that God has made it so clear. The principles are eternal truths and can be reintroduced into society and government.

Individuality

We must return to the proposition that all men are created in the image of God, each with a distinct purpose. As the Declaration of Independence declares, we have certain inalienable rights—life, liberty, the pursuit of happiness. We must reject the evolutionary philosophy that reduces man to a mass of chemicals without purpose or divine endowments.

Self-Government

We must take responsibility for our own actions. All government begins with the individual. Families and churches are also governments. We must remember that civil government is only one type of government with limited purposes, and stop relying on civil government to take care of all our needs.

Property

This principle teaches us to be good stewards of the gifts God has given. We need to recognize that God's gifts are both internal and external, with the gift of conscience being the most sacred. We must reject the idea that civil government is the owner and distributor of property and reaffirm that property is God's school of accountability for all mankind.

Unity and Union

We must acknowledge the right of men to associate voluntarily. The stress must be on internal unity of spirit, beliefs, and goals. Without internal unity, external union will be superficial and ineffective. Government must promote voluntary unity and union. Christians must resist any form of unbiblical coercion by civil government. Only then will we enjoy the self-government God intends for us to have.

Christian Character

We must realize that Christian character is essential for God's blessings on a nation. We also must stand firmly against the idea that private morality is different from public morality, that the private character of a public official has no effect on how he handles his public duties. Private morality eventually reveals itself publicly. We also must acknowledge that a people in a representative government receive the type of government they deserve. Character is not just a requirement for elected officials, but for the electorate as well.

Biblical Form of Government

We must appreciate the Biblical pattern of government upon which the United States was founded and fight to preserve representation, separation of powers, and the different levels of government within the federal system. Only then will tyranny be repulsed. We must recognize that although our structure remains the same as originally provided in the Constitution, our lack of Biblical principles has made the structure a hollow shell. We must infuse it once again with Biblical principles.

Sowing and Reaping

The key to the infusion of Biblical principles back into American society is the education system. It has been appropriated by humanist/socialist educators. We must reject the state-controlled system and opt for private, Biblically based education free from government regulation. The seeds of individuality, self-government, property, unity and union, Christian character, and a Christian form of government must be planted again in the hearts and minds of the current and future generations. Unless we take this task seriously, our Christian heritage will become a dim memory, and the influence of Biblical principles in our society will disintegrate further.

How will we accomplish all this? We must go back to God's principle of individuality. He has given each of us a specific calling in the work of restoration. We are not all called to be missionaries, teachers, or pastors. We are to find the calling God has on our lives, and if each individual fulfills his calling, God promises that He, through the Body of Christ, will supply every need.

No matter what our calling, we can actively support the callings of others, and we can actively resist the unbiblical principles and practices that have become part of our society and government.

In 1837, Noah Webster scrutinized the America in which he lived and commented sadly to an associate,

> *Principles*, Sir, are becoming corrupt, deeply corrupt; & unless the progress of corruption, & perversion of truth can be arrested, neither liberty nor property, will long be secure in this country. And a great evil is, that men of the first distinction seem, to a great extent, to be ignorant of the real, original causes of our public distresses.[1]

From our perspective in the twenty-first century, we may judge that Webster was too pessimistic. We look back on 1837 and see Biblical principles having a far greater impact on society than now. Yet it takes people like Webster to warn of the trends, and what he saw in 1837 eventually came to fruition. The seeds were being planted even then; the harvest was not long in coming.

I look at American society today. I can utter the same words Webster penned in 1837. Yet I see some glimmer of hope. Christians are finally becoming active again in the political realm. The Christian school and home school movements are burgeoning. All this activity has aroused opposition; America may be more bitterly divided now than it has been for over a century, and there is no guarantee of ultimate victory in this earthly realm. But God does reward and protect those who serve Him with a whole heart. He is looking for faithful individuals through whom He can work to make changes.

Jesus asked the best question for our times: "When the Son of Man comes, will He find faith on the earth?"[2] The book of Hebrews says, "Now faith is the assurance of things hoped for, the conviction of things not seen."[3] That is the kind of faith He seeks; it is the only kind of faith that will make a difference. May it be the faith that He finds.

ENDNOTES

Introduction

[1]Rev. Jedidiah Morse, *Election Sermon*, 25 April 1799 (Charlestown, MA, 1799).

Chapter 1

[1]The abolition movement in the nineteenth century began as a Christian attempt to remove slavery from America. Some of the abolitionists seemed, after a period of involvement, to reverse their priorities, making abolitionism a cause in itself and relegating the Christian basis of their abolitionism to a secondary role.
[2]The dominion mandate is found in Gen. 1:26-28.
[3]God's first instructions to Noah are found in Gen. 9:1-7. Many see in these instructions the Biblical origin of civil government in the sanction for executing a murderer.
[4]See the Sermon on the Mount in Matt. 5:13-16.
[5]See John 12:31.
[6]II Cor. 4:4 and Eph. 2:2, respectively.
[7]Is. 55:8-9.
[8]I Cor. 2:11.
[9]I Cor. 2:12.
[10]Prov. 1:7.

[11]Prov. 9:10.
[12]Deut. 6:6-9.
[13]Ps. 94:8-11.
[14]Ecc. 12:11-14.
[15]Jer. 3:15.
[16]Matt. 15:14.
[17]Rom. 1:18-23,25.
[18]I Cor. 1:20.
[19]I Cor. 2:6,8.
[20]I Cor. 2:12-16.
[21]I Cor. 3:20.
[22]Col. 2:2-3.
[23]Eph. 3:3,13 indicates that God can bring His Body into unity of faith, or belief, if His people will strive to maintain a unity of spirit. Christians may disagree, but they still can treat one another with the respect due a child of God.

Chapter 2

[1]Ps. 19:1-4.
[2]Rom. 1:20, which was described in the last chapter.
[3]Gal. 4:4.
[4]Gen. 1:26-28.
[5]II Cor. 4:7.
[6]I Cor. 12:14-18.
[7]I Cor. 12:21-25.
[8]I Cor. 12:27-30.
[9]Luke 1:3-4.
[10]Matt. 3:16-17.
[11]Acts 1:8.
[12]Didache, quoted in Eberhard Arnold, *The Early Christians after the Death of the Apostles* (Rifton, NY: Plough Publishing House, 1970), 182.

Chapter 3

[1]Quoted in Rosalie J. Slater, *Teaching and Learning America's Christian History: The Principle Approach* (San Francisco: Foundation for American Christian Education, 1965), 69.
[2]I Tim. 3:2-5.
[3]Gen. 2:16-17.
[4]Prov. 16:32.
[5]Acts 24:25.
[6]I Cor. 9:24-25.
[7]The entire passage is II Pet. 1:5-11.
[8]Gal. 5:24-25. The list of fruit is found in vv. 22-23.
[9]Eph. 4:29.
[10]Joseph Henry Thayer, *Greek-English Lexicon of the New Testament* (Grand Rapids: Associated Publishers and Authors, Inc.); reprint of 1889 edition.
[11]James 3:2,4-10.
[12]Gal. 3:1-3.
[13]Gal. 5:1,4.
[14]Col. 2:16-17,20-23.
[15]Rom. 12:2.
[16]II Cor. 10:5.
[17]Matt. 12:34-37.
[18]Heb. 12:14-15.
[19]Phil. 2:5-8.
[20]Heb. 4:12.
[21]Matt. 6:1-2,5,16.
[22]All the following quotes from Finney come from a sermon entitled, "True and False Conversion," in Charles G. Finney, *True and False Repentance* (Grand Rapids: Kregel Publications, 1966), 34-36.
[23]Eph. 4:26-27.
[24]I Cor. 15:10.
[25]Phil. 2:12-13.

²⁶Heb. 13:20-21.

²⁷See chapter 7 for details.

²⁸William Bradford, *The History of Plymouth Plantation* (Roslyn, NY: Walter J. Black, Inc., 1948), 74. This is a reprint edition of the original manuscript written by Bradford, Plymouth's governor for thirty-five years.

²⁹All quotes from *The Declaration of Independence*, 1776.

Chapter 4

¹This quote is taken straight from the dictionary definition of property. For a further explanation of Webster's Christian worldview and how it affected all his work, refer to K. Alan Snyder, *Defining Noah Webster: A Spiritual Biography* (Washington, DC: Allegiance Press, 2002).

²Gen. 1:28.

³Ps. 8:6.

⁴Matt. 25:14-30.

⁵ I Cor. 4:1-2.

⁶I Tim. 6:10.

⁷I Pet. 4:1-2.

⁸I Tim. 5:6,13-15.

⁹Prov. 11:15; 17:18.

¹⁰I Tim. 5:10.

¹¹Acts 6:3.

¹²Ecc. 12:7.

¹³Matt. 27:50.

¹⁴Rom. 8:16-17.

¹⁵Prov. 23:7.

¹⁶Phil. 4:8.

¹⁷Deut. 30:11.

¹⁸Deut. 30:19-20.

¹⁹I Tim. 4:1-2.

²⁰Deut. 8:18.

²¹Acts 2:44-45.

[22]Acts 4:32,34-35.

[23]Acts 5:1-4.

[24]Acts 5:8-9.

[25]Bradford, *Plymouth Plantation*, 151-152.

[26]Stephen Hopkins, "The Rights of the Colonies Examined," in Charles S. Hyneman and Donald S. Lutz, *American Political Writing during the Founding Era, 1760-1805*, 2 vols. (Indianapolis: Liberty Press, 1983), 1:46.

[27]All Madison quotes come from James Madison, "Property," *National Gazette*, 27 March 1792, found in *The Papers of James Madison*, Vol. 14 (Charlottesville: University of Virginia Press), 266-268.

[28]Acts 5:29.

[29]Rom. 14:22-23.

Chapter 5

[1]I Cor. 12:28-30.

[2]Amos 3:3.

[3]II Cor. 6:14-16.

[4]Prov. 17:17.

[5]Gen. 2:24; quoted by Jesus in Matt. 19:5 and Mark 10:7-8.

[6]Mark 10:9.

[7]I Cor. 1:10.

[8]Phil. 2:1-2.

[9]Eph. 4:1-3.

[10]Eph. 4:11-13.

[11]Prov. 18:24.

[12]Quoted in Verna M. Hall, comp., *The Christian History of the Constitution of the United States of America: Christian Self-Government with Union* (San Francisco: Foundation for American Christian Education, 1962; reprint ed., 1979), 323.

[13]Benjamin Franklin, *The Autobiography and Other Writings*, L. Jesse Lemisch, ed. (New York & Scarborough, Ontario: New American Library, 1961), 116-17.

[14]Quoted in Hall, *Christian History: Self-Government with Union*, 326.

[15]Proposal of the Massachusetts House of Representatives, 6 June 1765, quoted in Hall, *Christian History: Self-Government with Union*, 406.

[16]John Dickinson, "Farmer's Letter to the Inhabitants of the British Colonies," no. 7, quoted in Hall, *Christian History: Self-Government with Union*, 443.

[17]Dickinson, "Farmer's Letter," no. 12, quoted in Hall, *Christian History: Self-Government with Union*, 444.

[18]Dickinson, "Farmer's Letter," no. 12, quoted in Hall, *Christian History: Self-Government with Union*, 447.

[19]Quoted in David Ramsey, *History of the United States* (Philadelphia, 1816), in Verna M. Hall, comp., *The Christian History of the American Revolution: Consider and Ponder* (San Francisco: Foundation for American Christian Education, 1976), 467.

[20]The best book on the Christian nature of the Declaration is Gary Amos, *Defending the Declaration* (Brentwood, Tennessee: Wolgemuth and Hyatt, 1989).

[21]William Blackstone, *Commentaries*, quoted in Verna M. Hall, comp., *The Christian History of the Constitution of the United States of America: Christian Self-Government* (San Francisco: Foundation for American Christian Education, 1966), 142.

[22]Catherine Drinker Bowen, *Miracle at Philadelphia: The Story of the Constitutional Convention, May to September 1787* (Boston & Toronto: Little, Brown & Co., 1966), 126.

[23]Foremost in the literature on this subject is Charles Murray's *Losing Ground: American Social Policy*, 1950-

1980. Murray documents how the welfare state has hurt most the people it was intended to aid.

[24]Gen. 11:1-9.

Chapter 6

[1]Rom. 8:29.
[2]II Cor. 3:2-3.
[3]I John 4:7-8.
[4]I Cor. 13:4-7.
[5]Matt. 5:42-28.
[6]Rom. 5:8.
[7]Matt. 22:37-40.
[8]Rom. 2:11.
[9]Eph. 2:4.
[10]J. W. Jepson, ed., *A Digest of Finney's Systematic Theology* (1970), 26.
[11]John 17:17.
[12]John 14:6.
[13]John 16:13.
[14]Eph. 4:15,25.
[15]John 15:5.
[16]James 4:6,10.
[17]Mal. 3:6.
[18]James 1:17.
[19]Heb. 13:8 New International Version.
[20]I Pet. 1:15-16.
[21]Prov. 16:12.
[22]Prov. 20:28. The NIV translates this verse, "Love and faithfulness keep a king safe; through love his throne is made secure." Regardless which translation is used, the emphasis on character is unchanged.
[23]Prov. 28:16.
[24]Prov. 29:2,4.
[25]Prov. 24:23-25.

[26]Is. 10:1-2.
[27]Ex. 18:21.
[28]Deut. 1:16-17.
[29]Lev. 19:15.
[30]Deut. 16:19-20.
[31]Deut. 17:16-20.
[32]II Sam. 23:3-4.
[33]I Sam. 12:3-5.
[34]I Sam. 13:14.
[35]I Kings 10:6-9.
[36]I Kings 15:12-13; II Chron. 14:2.
[37]II Chron. 17:3-4,6. (NIV)
[38]II Chron. 19:6-7.
[39]II Kings 18:5.
[40]Dan. 6:3-4.
[41]I Kings 21:25.
[42]I Kings 21:20-24.
[43]Micah 3:9-12.
[44]Matt. 2:16-18.
[45]Matt. 14:1-12.
[46]Acts 12:21-23.
[47]Daniel Webster, quoted in Sidney Greenberg, ed., *A Treasury of the Art of Living* (Hartford: Hartmore House, 1963), 264, as cited in Philip C. Bom, *The Coming Century of Commonism* (Virginia Beach: Policy Books, 1992), 11.
[48]Hyneman and Lutz, *American Political Writing*, I, 38.
[49]Hyneman and Lutz, *American Political Writing*, I, 92.
[50]Bradford, *Plymouth Plantation*, 101.
[51]Bradford, *Plymouth Plantation*, 101-102.
[52]Bradford, *Plymouth Plantation*, 104.
[53]John Winthrop, "A Model of Christian Charity," in Alan Heimert and Alan Delbanco, *The Puritans in America* (Cambridge, MA: Harvard University Press, 1985), 90-91.

[54]Edmund S. Morgan, *The Puritan Dilemma: The Story of John Winthrop* (Boston: Little, Brown & Co., 1958), 58.

[55]Morgan, *Puritan Dilemma*, 62.

[56]Quoted in Pauline Maier, *The Old Revolutionaries: Political Lives in the Age of Samuel Adams* (New York: Vintage Books, 1982), 6.

[57]Maier, *Old Revolutionaries*, 11.

[58]Harry Alonzo Cushing, ed., *The Writings of Samuel Adams* (NY: G.P. Putnam's Sons, 1905), 4:124.

[59]Samuel Adams, "The Rights of the Colonists as Men, Christians, and Subjects," quoted in Hall, *Christian History: Christian Self-Government*, 365, 370.

[60]Quoted in Maier, *Old Revolutionaries*, 19.

[61]Maier, *Old Revolutionaries*, 26-27.

[62]Samuel Adams to Hannah Adams, 17 August 1780, quoted in Hall, *American Revolution: Consider and Ponder*, 82.

[63]Adams to Thomas Wells, 22 November 1780, quoted in Hall, *American Revolution: Consider and Ponder*, 82.

[64]Adams to Betsy Adams, 24 November 1780, quoted in Hall, *American Revolution: Consider and Ponder*, 84.

[65]John Adams, *Address as President to the Military*, in Charles Francis Adams, ed., *The Works of John Adams* (Boston: Little, Brown, & Co., 1854), 9:229.

[66]Charles Francis Adams, ed., *The Works of John Adams*, 9:401.

[67]L. H. Butterfield, ed., *The Diary and Autobiography of John Adams* (Cambridge, MA: The Belknap Press of Harvard University Press, 1962), 3:233-34.

[68]Quoted in Hall, *American Revolution: Consider and Ponder*, 604.

[69]Evidence of Washington's activity at the church is found in *Minutes of the Vestry, Truro Parish, Virginia, 1732-1785—Pohick Church* (Annandale, VA: Baptie Studios, Inc., 1974).

[70]John Eidsmoe, *Christianity and the Constitution: The Faith of Our Founding Fathers* (Grand Rapids: Baker Book House, 1987), 46.
[71]Eidsmoe, *Christianity and the Constitution*, 116.
[72]Eidsmoe, *Christianity and the Constitution*, 117.
[73]George Washington, "First Inaugural Address," 30 April 1789.
[74]George Washington, "Farewell Address," 1796.
[75]Abraham Lincoln, "Proclamation Appointing a National Fast Day," 30 March 1863.

Chapter 7

[1]I Pet. 2:13-14.
[2]I Tim. 2:1-2.
[3]Rom. 13:2.
[4]Rom. 13:4.
[5]Ex. 1:17,20.
[6]Daniel 3.
[7]Matt. 2:8,12.
[8]Acts 4:19-20.
[9]Acts 5:29.
[10]Luke 17:21. NIV
[11]John 18:36.
[12]John 19:11.
[13]Matt. 5:14-16.
[14]Deut. 1:13.
[15]Deut. 1:15.
[16]Judges 21:25.
[17]The following account is taken from I Sam. 8:4-22.
[18]Character qualification for elders and deacons can be found in I Tim. 3:1-13.
[19]Is. 33:22.
[20]See Helen Silving, "The Origins of the Magnae Cartae," 3 *Harvard Journal on Legislation* 117 (1965). Prof. Silving

concluded that the Magna Carta could be traced to Biblical origins.

[21]Richard L. Perry, ed., *Sources of Our Liberties: Documentary Origins of Individual Liberties in the United States Constitution and Bill of Rights*, rev. ed. (Buffalo, NY: William S. Hein & Co., Inc., 1991), 57.

[22]*Fundamental Orders of Connecticut*, 1639.

[23]Donald S. Lutz, "The Relative Influence of European Writers on Late Eighteenth-Century American Political Thought," *The American Political Science Review* 78 (1984): 192.

[24]For a fuller treatment of Locke's linkage of the Bible with his politics, see Amos, *Defending the Declaration*.

[25]Charles de Secondat Montesquieu, *The Spirit of Laws*, 1748.

[26]Alexander Hamilton, James Madison, John Jay, *The Federalist Papers*, no. 41, Clinton Rossiter, ed. (New York: New American Library, 1961), 262-263.

[27]Thomas Jefferson, quoted in W. David Stedman and LaVaughn G. Lewis, eds., *Our Ageless Constitution* (Asheboro, NC: W. David Stedman Associates, 1987), 265.

[28]Stedman and Lewis, *Ageless Constitution*, 266.

[29]Quoted in Kerry L. Morgan, "A Constitutional Presidency," *Journal of Christian Jurisprudence* 7 (1988): 62-63.

[30]Morgan, "Constitutional Presidency," 63.

[31]Quoted in Bettina B. Greaves, comp., *Free Market Economics: A Basic Reader* (Irvington-on-Hudson, NY: Foundation for Economic Freedom, 1975), 227-228. Taken from Edward S. Ellis, comp., *The Life of Colonel David Crockett* (Philadelphia: Porter & Coates, 1884).

[32]Hamilton, Madison, Jay, *Federalist Papers*, no. 78, Rossiter, ed., 467.

[33]Hamilton, Madison, Jay, *Federalist Papers*, no. 78, Rossiter, ed., 468-469.

[34]Hamilton, Madison, Jay, *Federalist Papers*, no. 78, Rossiter, ed., 465.

[35]Hamilton, Madison, Jay, *Federalist Papers*, no. 78, Rossiter, ed., 465-466.

[36]Hamilton, Madison, Jay, *Federalist Papers*, no. 33, Rossiter, ed., 205.

[37]Gary Amos, "A Limited National Congress," *Journal of Christian Jurisprudence* 7 (1988): 120.

[38]Eidsmoe, *Christianity and the Constitution*, 388.

[39]Both Douglas's and Berger's observations are found in John W. Whitehead, *The Second American Revolution* (Elgin, IL: David C. Cook Publishing Company, 1982), 213.

[40]Forrest McDonald, *A Constitutional History of the United States* (New York: Franklin Watts, 1982), 223.

[41]Civil Rights Act of 1964, Title VII.

[42]"America on the Couch," *National Right to Life News*, vol. 19, no. 12 (21 July 1992), 2.

[43]Wanda Franz, "A Confused and Arrogant Supreme Court Reaffirms the 'Right to Abortion,'" *National Right to Life News*, vol. 19, no. 12 (21 July 1992), 3.

Chapter 8

[1]Gal. 6:7-8.

[2]Luke 8:4-15.

[3]These quotes taken from "Old South Leaflets," from a letter dated 26 September 1642, found in Hall, *Christian History: Christian Self-Government*, 240b.

[4]Samuel L. Blumenfeld, *Is Public Education Necessary?* (Boise, ID: The Paradigm Company, 1981), 42-43.

[5]Quoted in Blumenfeld, *Is Public Education Necessary?* 82. Blumenfeld's book provides the basis for this entire discussion.

⁶A.G. Keller and Maurice Davie, eds., *Selected Essays of William Graham Sumner*, I (Yale University Press, 1934), 301, quoted in C. Gregg Singer, *A Theological Interpretation of American History* (Nutley, NJ: The Craig Press, 1978), 107.

⁷Letter from Holmes to John C.H. Wu, 26 August 1926, in Harry C. Shriver, ed., *Justice Oliver Wendell Holmes: His Book Notices and Uncollected Letters and Papers*, 187, quoted in *Whitehead, The Second American Revolution*, 51.

⁸Quoted in *Whitehead, Second American Revolution*, 52.

⁹For an excellent historical study of the influence of Freudianism on American society, see E. Fuller Torrey, *Freudian Fraud* (NY: Harper-Collins, 1992).

¹⁰I Cor. 6:9-11.

¹¹William Kirk Kilpatrick, *Psychological Seduction* (Nashville: Thomas Nelson Publishers, 1983), 23.

¹²Kilpatrick, *Psychological Seduction*, 13-14.

¹³Herbert Schlossberg and Marvin Olasky, *Turning Point: A Christian Worldview Declaration* (Westchester, IL: Crossway Books, 1987), 31-32.

¹⁴Humanist Manifesto I, which first appeared in *The New Humanist*, vol. 6, no. 3 (May/June 1933).

¹⁵John Dewey, *Democracy and Education* (NY: Macmillan, The Free Press, 1916), 19.

¹⁶John Dewey, "My Pedagogic Creed," in *Dewey on Education*, with an introduction and notes by Martin S. Dworkin, *Classics in Education*, No. 3 (NY: Teachers College Press, 1959), 25-26.

¹⁷John Dewey, *The School and Society*, Jo Ann Boydston, ed. (Carbondale & Edwardsville, IL: Southern Illinois University Press, 1980), 19.

¹⁸Katherine Camp Mayhew and Anna Camp Edwards, *The Dewey School*, quoted in Blumenfeld, *NEA: Trojan Horse*, 54.

[19]Blair Adams, *Who Owns the Children? Public Compulsion, Private Responsibility, and the Dilemma of Ultimate Authority*, 5th ed. (Waco, TX: Truth Forum, 1991), 11.

[20]Paul C. Vitz, *Censorship: Evidence of Bias in Our Children's Textbooks* (Ann Arbor, MI: Servant Books, 1986), 1.

[21]Vitz, *Censorship*, 11.

[22]Vitz, *Censorship*, 16.

[23]Vitz, *Censorship*, 3.

[24]Vitz, *Censorship*, 41.

[25]Vitz, *Censorship*, 34.

[26]Vitz, *Censorship*, 35.

[27]All of the following resolutions are taken from the NEA's own magazine, *NEA Today*, September 1997. Most of the NEA's resolutions on the issues discussed here have not changed in years; resolutions noted here from 1997 also reflect the current stands of the NEA.

Conclusion

[1]Noah Webster to Charles Chauncey, 17 October 1837, *Chauncey Family Papers*, Manuscripts and Archives, Yale University Library, New Haven, Connecticut.

[2]Luke 18:8.

[3]Heb. 11:1.

BIBLIOGRAPHY

Adams, Blair. *Who Owns the Children? Public Compulsion, Private Responsibility, and the Dilemma of Ultimate Authority.* 5th ed. Waco, TX: Truth Forum, 1991.

Amos, Gary. *Defending the Declaration.* Brentwood, TN: Wolgemuth and Hyatt, 1989.

_____. "A Limited National Congress." *Journal of Christian Jurisprudence* 7 (1988):99-125.

Arnold, Eberhard. *The Early Christians after the Death of the Apostles.* Rifton, NY: Plough Publishing House, 1970.

Bowen, Catherine Drinker. *Miracle at Philadelphia: The Story of the Constitutional Convention, May to September 1787.* Boston & Toronto: Little, Brown & Co., 1966.

Blumenfeld, Samuel L. *Is Public Education Necessary?* Boise, ID: The Paradigm Co., 1981.

_____. *NEA: Trojan Horse in American Education.* Boise, ID: The Paradigm Co., 1984.

Bradford, William. *The History of Plymouth Plantation*. Reprint ed. Roslyn, NY: Walter J. Black, Inc., 1948.

Eidsmoe, John. *Christianity and the Constitution: The Faith of Our Founding Fathers*. Grand Rapids: Baker Book House, 1987.

Finney, Charles G. *True and False Repentance.* Reprint ed. Grand Rapids: Kregel Publications, 1966.

Franklin, Benjamin. *The Autobiography and Other Writings*. L. Jesse Lemisch, ed. New York & Scarborough, Ontario: New American Library, 1961.

Franz, Wanda. "A Confused and Arrogant Supreme Court Reaffirms the 'Right to Abortion.'" *National Right to Life News*. Vol. 19, no. 12 (21 July 1992).

Greaves, Bettina B., comp. *Free Market Economics: A Basic Reader*. Irvington-on-Hudson, NY: Foundation for Economic Freedom, 1975.

Hall, Verna M., comp. *The Christian History of the American Revolution: Consider and Ponder*. San Francisco: Foundation for American Christian Education, 1976.

_____., comp. *The Christian History of the Constitution of the United States of America: Christian Self-Government*. San Francisco: Foundation for American Christian Education, 1966.

_____., comp. *The Christian History of the Constitution of the United States of America: Christian Self-Government with Union*. San Francisco: Foundation for American Christian Education, 1962; reprint ed., 1979.

Hamilton, Alexander, James Madison, and John Jay. *The Federalist Papers*. Clinton Rossiter, ed. NY: New American Library, 1961.

Heimert, Alan, and Alan Delbanco. *The Puritans in America*. Cambridge, MA: Harvard University Press, 1985.

Hyneman, Charles S., and Donald S. Lutz. *American Political Writing during the Founding Era*, 1760-1805. 2 vols. Indianapolis: Liberty Press, 1983.

Jepson, J.W., ed. *A Digest of Finney's Systematic Theology*, 1970.

Kilpatrick, William Kirk. *Psychological Seduction*. Nashville: Thomas Nelson Publishers, 1983.

Lutz, Donald S. "The Relative Influence of European Writers on Late Eighteenth-Century American Political Thought." *The American Political Science Review* 78 (1984):189-197.

Maier, Pauline. *The Old Revolutionaries: Political Lives in the Age of Samuel Adams*. NY: Vintage Books, 1982.

McDonald, Forrest. *A Constitutional History of the United States*. NY: Franklin Watts, 1982.

Minutes of the Vestry, Truro Parish, Virginia, 1732-1785— Pohick Church. Annandale, VA: Baptie Studios, Inc., 1974.

Morgan, Edmund S. *The Puritan Dilemma: The Story of John Winthrop*. Boston: Little, Brown & Co., 1958.

Morgan, Kerry L. "A Constitutional Presidency." *Journal of Christian Jurisprudence* 7 (1988):45-70.

Morse, Jedidiah. *Election Sermon*, 25 April 1799. Charlestown, MA, 1799.

Murray, Charles. *Losing Ground: American Social Policy*, 1950-1980. NY: Basic Books, 1984.

NEA Today, September 1997.

The Papers of James Madison. Vol. 14. Charlottesville: University of Virginia Press.

Perry, Richard, ed. *Sources of Our Liberties: Documentary Origins of Individual Liberties in the United States Constitution and Bill of Rights*. Revised edition. Buffalo, NY: William S. Hein & Co., Inc., 1991.

Reeves, Thomas C. *A Question of Character: A Life of John F. Kennedy*. NY: The Free Press, 1991.

Schlossberg, Herbert, and Marvin Olasky. *Turning Point: A Christian Worldview Declaration*. Westchester, IL: Crossway Books, 1987.

Silving, Helen. "The Origins of the Magnae Cartae." 3 *Harvard Journal on Legislation* 117 (1965):117-131.

Singer, C. Gregg. *A Theological Interpretation of American History*. Nutley, NJ: The Craig Press, 1978.

Slater, Rosalie J. *Teaching and Learning America's Christian History: The Principle Approach*. San Francisco: Foundation for American Christian Education, 1965.

Snyder, K. Alan. *Defining Noah Webster: A Spiritual Biography*. Washington, DC: Allegiance Press, 2002.

Stedman, W. David, and LaVaughn G. Lewis, eds. *Our Ageless Constitution*. Asheboro, NC: W. David Stedman Associates, 1987.

Torrey, E. Fuller. *Freudian Fraud*. NY: Harper-Collins, 1992.

Vitz, Paul C. *Censorship: Evidence of Bias in Our Children's Textbooks*. Ann Arbor, MI: Servant Books, 1986.

Whitehead, John W. *The Second American Revolution*. Elgin, IL: David C. Cook Publishing Co., 1982.

INDEX

CPSIA information can be obtained
at www.ICGtesting.com
Printed in the USA
LVHW031504290120
645190LV00004B/326